Sanekata-shū:

The Personal Poetry Collection of Fujiwara no Sanekata

Revised Edition

Translated and Edited by

T. E. McAuley

Copyright © 2021 by T. E. McAuley

All rights reserved. No part of this book may be reproduced or used in any manner without written permission of the copyright owner except for the use of quotations in a book review.

ISBN 978-0-9956948-3-5 (ebook)
ISBN 978-0-9956948-4-2 (paperback)
ISBN 978-0-9956948-5-9 (hardback)

Published by www.wakapoetry.net

Table of Contents

Preface to the Revised Edition i

Introduction iii

Acknowledgements x

Sanekata's Collection 1

References 167

Index 168

Index of First Lines 174

Preface to the Revised Edition

I think that perhaps there has never been a writer who has been completely satisified with the supposed 'final' version of their works: there is always one thing or another that one is tempted to fix or change to make them better. I, of course, am no exception to this and so, while I was happy, and still am, with the first edition of this book, there were still some elements of it which, given an opportunity, I felt could be improved, or altered, to create a version of it which would be more useful and allow readers to derive more from their reading of Sanekata's poems.

Being able to revisit a book one has already written is, of course, something of a luxury, and one which is rarely afforded a busy academic who has to be constantly thinking of the next new publication rather than looking back at those which have already been entrusted to the public. The COVID-19 pandemic, however, has disrupted many aspects of everyone's lives, and meant that, in my case, the ability and time to pursue new research has been severely curtailed. Rather than do nothing, though, I decided to devote some time to taking another look at *Sanekata-shū*, and doing what I could to improve it. In addition, having had the experience of finalising the manuscript of my translation of *Roppyakuban uta'awase* ('The Poetry Contest in Six Hundred Rounds') (McAuley, 2020a), I wanted to put some of the lessons I had learned into practice. This new, revised, edition is the result of those efforts, and this preface my chance to outline what the revisions are, and are not.

First of all, I have not extensively revised the translations of the poems, beyond making a few minor changes to wording where I have thought of a different phrase, or to eliminate typographical errors which escaped the revision process when the initial version of the text was being produced. This is not because I do not believe the translations could be improved – they undoubtedly can – but because the process of revising them, once started, is something I would find difficult to stop, so for better or worse the translations must stand on their merits.

I have, however, substantially revised and increased the annotations for the translations and headnotes. They now provide much more detailed information about the personages Sanekata mentions, the poetic diction he uses, and the court events in which he took part. This will, I hope, enable readers to understand much better who the people were in Sanekata's life, why he expresses himself in poetry the way that he does, and what would have happened at the functions he attended.

I have also included the Japanese script version of the poems, and for many other terms mentioned in the text For readers more familiar with the world of *waka*, I felt this would make the book more useful as a reference work, while for others I hope that seeing what the poems look like in their original script adds a pleasant aesthetic touch. A further change is that I have altered the transcription system used for the Japanese versions of the poems. In the first edition of the book, the transcription system attempted to replicate the pronunciation of Japanese at the time the poems were composed, whereas in this edition the system reflects the pronunciation of the modern language.

While the linguistic purist in me balks at this change slightly, the simple fact is that if anyone except the most specialised of specialists discusses, or recites, premodern *waka* today, they do so in modern Japanese. Thus it seems churlish to place obstacles to doing this in my readers' way in the Quixotic cause of linguistic faithfulness. Experts will know how to read the poems with a Heian pronunciation if they need to, regardless of the transcription supplied; for others, a modern one permits better access to the world of *waka* beyond this book – a world which I hope some will feel encouraged to explore. To aid in this there is also a new list of references at the end of the book: it is brief and limited to those works which I mention in the introduction and annotations, and those are deliberately few in number, and, at the risk of self-aggrandisement, contains a couple of my own works, but I hope this will give readers a place to start a further exploration of premodern Japanese literature and literary studies.

Finally, as this version of the book, unlike the first, is intended to be available in both hard-copy as well as electronic format, the former versions will also include a general index and an index of first lines to make quick reference easier. My hope is that these features will, again, make the book more useful for a wider range of readers.

T.E.McAuley
Sheffield
June 2021

Introduction

In the mid-tenth century, Japan was nominally an empire ruled by a divine sovereign from the imperial capital of Heian-kyō 平安京 (present day Kyoto). From his palace, the emperor oversaw a complicated structure of bureaucratic ministries and offices, and despatched governors to the far-flung provinces to ensure that his edicts were obeyed, and that taxes and tithes flowed without interruption to the state's coffers. His officials were chosen from among the great families of the land, whose sons attended the imperial university, took its examinations and were appointed to government positions on the basis of merit. Meanwhile, the daughters of great houses were placed in court service and became consorts or concubines, depending upon their prestige and fortune.

That, at least, is the idealised version, but the reality is far more complex. Japan had imported much of its governing structures from China, but, like Heian-kyō itself, which was intended to be a smaller-scale duplicate of the Tang capital of Chang'an, but never fully completed, the importation was never total, and subject to extensive modification. The emperor always reigned, but rarely ruled; government positions were as likely to be filled on the basis of family connections as on merit, and were increasingly bypassed as they became mere sinecures; appointments to provincial governorships were often delegated to lower-ranking subordinates to avoid years spent away from the civilised surroundings of the capital, and the government eventually became insolvent as tax revenues were diverted into private hands, or never left the provinces. Finally, towards the end of the twelfth century, the imperial government ceased to have any meaningful control over the country at all as the rise of the provincial samurai warrior class rendered it irrelevant and ushered in a period of military rule which was to last until the mid-nineteenth century.

While the seeds of the demise of court control had already been sown by the mid-tenth century, for the court aristocracy of the time life was stable and prosperous, allowing them the leisure to pursue literary and cultural activities. The result was a great cultural flowering, producing a significant quantity of both poetry and prose, which was to influence ideas about life, love and literature for centuries to come. In particular, with the completion of the first imperial poetry anthology, *Kokinwakashū* 古今和歌集 ('Collection of Japanese Poems, Ancient and Modern') between 915–920, the nobility had both a confident assertion of the critical value and formal qualities of *waka* 和歌 ('Japanese poetry') from the collection's preface by its most influential compiler, Ki no Tsurayuki 紀貫之 (ca. 872–945), and, from its contents, model examples of poetic topics and suitable diction.

That poetry would be granted the status of this imperial recognition was, perhaps, inevitable, given the centrality of poetic composition to aristocratic life. A poem was the standard means by which people expressed their emotional responses to both nature and events in their lives, and had been for centuries. Indeed, it would not be too much of an over-statement to say that it would be almost impossible for anyone to function as a full member of aristocratic society if they lacked the ability to compose a poem when the need arose; while there were people whose skills in poetic composition were acknowledged, it was not the preserve of a literary elite, it was simply something that everyone did. Of course, the vast majority of these compositions were ephemeral and have not survived the centuries to the present day, but as the status granted by acceptance of someone's poem for inclusion in an imperial anthology became clear, it was in individual poets' interests, and that of their families, to retain and collect particularly good compositions so that they might be reviewed for future anthologies, and form a poetic inheritance for the future. The result of this was that anyone with any pretensions to poetic skill would have a *shikashū* 私家集, a personal collection of their own poetry, often inspired by and functioning as a commentary on, the events of their own lives. Some of these, by poets whose abilities were recognised by future generations, and who have been blessed by good fortune, have survived to the present day. The *Sanekata-shū* 実方集 is one among them.

Fujiwara no Sanekata

Today, Sanekata is, perhaps, best known in Japan as one of the poets selected by Fujiwara no Teika 藤原定家 (1162–1241) for inclusion in his *Ogura hyakunin isshu* 小倉百人一首 ('Little Storehouse Collection of One Hundred Poems by One Hundred Poets'),[1] a collection of poems which forms the basis for *karuta*, a traditional New Year entertainment in which cards with the second half of the *hyakunin isshu* poems written on them are placed before two players, while a third reads out the first half of each poem in turn. The players have to quickly spot the corresponding card and seize it before their opponent, resulting in much lunging and enjoyment. A corollary of this, however, is that the *hyakunin isshu* poems are probably the most widely known and memorised of all premodern *waka*, and the names of their composers, if not much more in many cases, are known, too.

---

[1] This collection has been translated into English multiple times, most recently by Frank Watson Watson F (2020) *One Hundred Leaves: A new annotated translation of the Hyakunin Isshu*. Plum White Press. and Peter McMillan McMillan P (2010) *One Hundred Poets, One Poem Each: A Translation of the Ogura Hyakunin Isshu*. New York: Columbia University Press..

In Sanekata's case there is, in fact, little detail to be known: records of the exact year of his birth have not survived, but it is thought to have been around 958, as he was said to have been forty at the time of his death in early 999. He was a member of the Fujiwara family, a sprawling clan with many different branches, one of which, through judicious marriage to the imperial family, was to assume *de facto* control of Japan and dominate its government in later years. Sanekata, in fact, came from this branch, but was not one of its most fortunate members, and a reputation for bad luck dogs him even now.

Sanekata's father, Sadatoki 定時 (dates unknown), was the eldest son of Fujiwara no Morotada 藤原師尹 (920–969), while his mother was a daughter of Minamoto no Masazane 源雅信 (920–993). Both Morosada and Masazane were eventually to reach one of the highest government positions, Minister of the Left, in 969 and 977 respectively, and one would think that with these strong familial connections Sanekata's future would have been assured. Sadatoki, however, died young, and Masazane was unwilling to offer the boy his support, so he was adopted by his uncle, Naritoki 済時 (941–995). Naritoki, of course, had his own sons' careers to consider and so Sanekata had to make do with what political capital his uncle was prepared to expend on him.

This support was sufficient to secure him a position in the palace guards in his mid-teens, and it was there that he was to spend almost his entire court career, rising eventually to the position of Middle Captain of the Inner Palace Guards, Left Division (*Sakonoe chūjō* 左近衛中将) in 994, the year after he had been raised to Junior Fourth Rank, Upper Grade, a status which placed him on the threshold of admittance to the most senior ranks of the upper nobility. For reasons which still remain obscure, however, at the beginning of 995 he was demoted by being appointed Governor of Michinoku 陸奥 province in the north of Japan, and a few months later suffered a further loss when Naritoki died in an outbreak of plague which struck the capital. It was not until his mourning for his adoptive father ended later that year that he left for his provincial post. It was there that he remained, and in early 999, as he was riding past Kasashima dōso 笠島道祖 shrine (now Saeno 佐倍乃 shrine) in Natori, his horse collapsed and rolled over him, resulting in his death. He was buried in Michinoku, far from his birthplace in the capital, and his grave can still be found there.

These are the bare bones of Sanekata's life: he left no diary, unlike many of his contemporaries, and aside from brief mentions of him in others' writings we have only one other source of information about him: his poetry as preserved in his personal collection. From this we know that he corresponded with a large number of court ladies and, from the tone of many of the poems, was intimate with many of them. He also took part in many different court entertainments and activities, as would have been expected of a man of his rank. This dearth of information has meant that in the years after his death a range of anecdotes began to be told about him (including that he was demoted to Provincial Governor and sent off to the provinces after getting into an argument with another courtier about poetry and knocking his cap of rank off, resulting in the emperor telling him to, 'Go and see some poetic locations for yourself!'), until the legend eclipsed the man to a great extent. He became a figure of passion and tragedy, much like Ariwara no Narihira 在原業平 (825–880) a hundred years earlier, and is even cited as one of the real-life models which Murasaki Shikibu 紫式部 drew upon when forming her image of the protagonist of *Genji monogatari* 源氏物語 ('The Tale of Genji').

This reputation, coupled with his undoubted poetic abilities, meant that from the third imperial anthology *Shūiwakashū* 拾遺和歌集 ('Collection of Gleanings of Japanese Poetry'; 1005–11), his poems began to be selected for inclusion, and he eventually had 67 of his works included in a variety of anthologies, a more than respectable total for any poet. By the early twelfth century, this meant that his fame was such that he was counted among the 36 Later Poetic Immortals (*Chūko sanjū rokkasen* 中古三十六歌仙), by Fujiwara no Norikane 藤原範兼 (1107–65), and the famous monk-poet Saigyō 西行 (1118-1190), who travelled widely in Japan, composed this poem on seeing Sanekata's grave:

> *When he was passing through the fields, having gone down to Michinoku, he saw an impressive tomb and asked whose it was; he was told it was the tomb of 'the Captain'. On asking which Captain, he was told they meant Sanekata; it was winter, and he absently noted the miscanthus grass all around was withered by the frost and, feeling that there was nothing [there] that suited the time…*

くちもせぬその名ばかりをとゞめをきてかれ野のすゝきかたみとぞみる

kuchi mo senu	Imperishable
sono na bakari o	His name alone
todomeokite	Remains left here;
kareno no sususki	The frost-burned field of miscanthus
katami to zo miru	Will be my keepsake.

(SKKS VIII: 793)

A further monument, of course, is his poems, as included in his personal collection, and presented here.

Sanekata-shū and its Translation

Sanekata's personal collection contains 348 poems. Not all of them are by him: some are poems by other people, both men and women, with whom Sanekata corresponded. Approximately half the poems can broadly be described as love poems, a quarter refer in one way or another to court activities in which Sanekata took part, and the final quarter are more personal – either communications with friends or family, or, not surprisingly given his circumstances, laments over his misfortunes. The vast majority come with a headnote explaining the context in which the poem was composed, and aiding in their interpretation. Unlike the formal topics (*dai* 題) of later poetry, however, these are almost all linked to social interactions Sanekata had with others, and serve to demonstrate how intimately poetic composition was linked with all the minutiae of everyday aristocratic life in Heian Japan.

Throughout the collection, Sanekata deploys all the techniques of the Heian poet: seasonal references, wordplay, *utamakura* 歌枕 (references to locations associated with particular qualities) and *makura kotoba* 枕詞 (literally 'pillow words' – conventionalised images and expressions used to describe particular nouns). While the poetry of Sanekata's time does not display the level of intertextuality which was to become a feature of *waka* composition by the end of the Heian period in the late 1100s, it is still poetry written by a man deeply familiar with his national canon – and who expected the readers of his poems to have a similar level of familiarity: to be able to interpret his wordplays, to identify passing references to other poems, poets or writings, and understand the conventional connotations of the seasons, and their associated plants and animals. Equally, because it was customary to refer to men by title rather than name, and it was taboo to write the name of any noble woman, other than an empress, with the passage of a thousand years, we now simply do know who some of Sanekata's poetic correspondents were, although their identity would have been clear to his contemporaries.

These features mean that Sanekata's poetry and, indeed, many *waka*, can be difficult to understand fully without study and the provision of varying quantities of background information, which can obscure and delay the direct appreciation of the poems' literary qualities. In addition, the thirty-one syllable brevity of the originals often contains multiple layers of meanings provided by wordplays and the extended connotations of poetic expressions. Occasionally this means that a poem can be simultaneously a lyric statement about nature and, for example, a personal and passionate declaration of love – something which it is impossible to replicate simply in English.

Translators of *waka*, then, must make a number of decisions about their translation strategies in dealing with the poems.[2] First, should the thirty-one syllable count and 'lines' of 5–7–5–7–7 syllables of the originals be replicated in English? Doing so emphasises the consistency of the form, and imposes a degree of discipline, but my own feeling is that the key function of this structure in Japanese was the mark texts in this pattern as poems, and that if the English versions are marked as such through separation into lines and verses, there is little to be gained by replicating the Japanese syllable count. In the translations, here, therefore, I have not attempted to replicate the syllable count, but do present the translations as five lines, each one matched against one in the transcribed Japanese versions of the poems.

Second, should the grammatical or imagistic structures of the originals be prioritised? Japanese is a Subject-Object-Verb language, which places modifying elements before the nouns they modify. This means that if a translation closely follows the grammatical structure of the original poem, it will almost always present the images it expresses to the reader in the reverse order to that of the original work. Alternatively, following the order of the original's images involves distorting the grammatical structure of the source. In the translations here, I have chosen to follow the latter strategy as far as possible, except where it would mean compromising the sense of the original poem completely, on the grounds that part of the pleasure of *waka* is in following the unfolding images through the poems as they qualify and expand each other.

Third, how far should wordplays be explicated? Full explication, while educational, tends to produce lengthy and convoluted expressions, which does not correspond to the originals' brevity. In the translations here, therefore, I have followed a dual strategy of expanding some wordplays in the translations, while providing annotations to explicate others, with the aim of keeping the direct style of the originals as far as possible.

Finally, diction: *waka* utilised a limited range of expressions which were accepted as being poetic, and part of a poem's impact and pleasure was provided by an understanding of the poetic connotations attached to individual nouns or expressions. The translator is, therefore, faced with the choice of whether restrict the translations in a similar fashion to the originals – to always translate individual words the same way – as a method of demonstrating the links between poems, but which might produce repetitive English; or, varying the English translations, at the cost of obscuring how individual words were used in multiple poems and linked them together. In the translations here, I have attempted to steer a middle

---

[2] For a more detailed discussion of the translation of Japanese *waka* poetry than I have space for here, see McAuley TE (2020b) The Power of Translation: Issues in the translation of premodern Japanese waka. *Waseda RILAS Journal* 8: 1-19..

course between these two extremes and avoid overly repetitive translations, but also too great a variety of diction.

    Overall, my intention has been to attempt to produce translations which can be read and enjoyed as English poems first, but then delved into more deeply with the aid of annotations if desired. I hope I have been generally successful in this aim, but am certain that it has not been achieved in all cases. Nevertheless, through this complete translation of Sanekata's private collection of poetry, I hope that readers will gain a sense of the man, his interests and his world, and be able to see how much we have in common with the nobility of Heian Japan, even though we are separated by such a gulf of time, culture and history.

Acknowledgements

In 2001, as a way of making a contribution to the Japan 2001 Festival marking 100 years of diplomatic relations between Japan and the UK, I was encouraged to join together both the online environment and premodern poetry in a project to translate 2001 *waka* in the course of the year, circulate them via a mailing list, and make them available online. The result was the *Japan 2001 Waka* website, which was completed in early 2002. After such an intensive period of translation, however, I found I had no wish to stop and so continued translating, circulating and uploading poems. By 2015, the site had almost doubled in size with over 3500 poems available, but its structure had become unwieldy and difficult to monitor, so it was time for a change.

The result was the transformation of *Japan 2001 Waka* into WakaPoetry.net (www.wakapoetry.net) in early 2016, with additional content to provide further background information on the world of *waka* – in particular the plants referenced in the eighth century *Man'yōshū* poetry anthology, and the botanical gardens in Japan which display them, which are the focus of part of my current research. In the discussions surrounding the site's relaunch, however, it was suggested that some readers might want to be able to enjoy *waka* on the go via their preferred e-readers, which provided the impetus for the creation of a series of volumes to make the translations more widely available. The *Sanekata-shū*, as a self-contained and focussed unit, and a work which has not been translated in its entirety before is the first of these works – there will be more to follow.

Many people have contributed to the creation of this book – too many to thank properly in full – but special mention must go to colleagues at both the University of Limerick and the School of East Asian Studies at the University of Sheffield who encouraged and appreciated both my initial and later attempts at *waka* translation. Next, thanks are owed to all the many people who have corresponded with me over the years via *Japan 2001 Waka* seeking information and advice about Japanese poetry, and who have challenged me to continue translating – without this stimulation, I am not sure I would have continued this long.

I must also express thanks to a few named individuals: to Glenn Hook, for encouraging the initial project application which led to *Japan 2001 Waka*; to Peter Matanle, for championing academic self-publishing; to Chris Reed for designing the original *Japan 2001 Waka* and producing this ebook – without your support it would not be here.

I must also express my thanks to and acknowledge the support of the Great Britain Sasakawa Foundation. It was the Foundation's financial support which made the original *Japan 2001 Waka* possible, and a further grant which laid the groundwork for *WakaPoetry.net* as well as the production of this work.

    Finally, to my long-suffering family, who have accepted me burying myself a thousand years in the past of a country on the far side of the world: I could not have done this without you.

Sanekata's Collection

1

On the day when a messenger was sent with offerings to the Usa Shrine,¹ remembering the past when I had done the job:²

むかしみし心ばかりをしるべにて思ひぞをくるいきの松原

mukashi mishi
kokoro bakari o
shirube nite
omoi zo okuru
*iki no matsubara*³

Sights seen in times long past:
Those feelings alone, are
My guide
To send my thoughts through
The groves of living pine.

---

¹ The Usa Shrine 宇佐神宮 was located in the province of Buzen 豊前 in the north-east of Kyushu. It is the principal shrine to the deity Hachiman 八幡, one of the major deities of the Shinto pantheon, and the divine guardian of Japan who sent the 'divine wind' (*kamikaze* 神風) which destroyed the Mongol invasion fleet in the fourteenth century. Hachiman is actually a combination of Emperor Ōjin 応神天, the fifteenth emperor, and his mother, Empress Jingū 神宮皇后, who legendarily carried him in her womb for three years while she led Japanese forces in the conquest of Korea, and is regarded as the deity of writing, culture, war, divination and protection. Hachiman's antecedents as an Imperial ancestor and his role as a guardian meant that annual offerings were made to him by the court.

² Court records show that Sanekata was imperial messenger to the Usa Shrine in 983.

³ The phrase *iki no matsubara* いきの松原, which I have translated here as 'groves of living pine', was a set poetic expression for the province of Chikuzen 筑前 in the north of modern Fukuoka 福岡 prefecture in northern Kyushu, which one would have had to travel through to reach Usa Shrine.

2

In the year[1] in which Lord Tamemasa was Imperial messenger to the festival at Iwashimizu Hachiman Shrine,[2] on the day after I been a dancer there and was returning home with others, on wearing blossom[3] in our hair:

桂川かざしの花の影みえしきのふのふちぞ今日は戀しき

katsuragawa	By the River Katsura[4]
kazashi no hana no	The blossom in your hair
kage mieshi	Shining I saw:
kinō no fuchi zo	The tranquil, violet deeps of
kyō wa koishiki	yesterday
	Are dear, indeed, to me today.

---

[1] Sanekata is thought to have been a dancer at this festival in 983 and/or 984.

[2] Iwashimizu Hachiman Shrine 岩清水八幡宮 was located to the south of the capital and was established in 859. At the time of this poem's writing it had close connections with the court and often received noble patronage; from the end of the eleventh century, however, it came to be seen as the patron shrine of the warrior Minamoto clan and began to receive the support of the samurai class. The shrine festival referred to here took place at the beginning of the Third Month.

[3] For the festival, dancers would wear cherry blossom, while an imperial messenger would wear wisteria (*fuji* 藤). In the poem, Sanekata plays with words by referring to the 'deeps'(*fuchi* 渕) of the river: *fuji* and *fuchi* were written identically in old Japanese as ふち, so he combines the river with the (violet) wisteria in his friend's hair.

[4] The Katsura River (*katsuragawa* 桂川) flows south from Arashiyama 嵐山 to the north of Kyoto, along the city's western side. The Iwashimizu Hachiman Shrine is located at the point where it joins the Kizu 木津 and Uji 宇治 rivers, and transforms into the Yodo 淀 River.

3

On a pine tree on the rocks, while at the Shirakawa estate.[1]

いにしへの種としみれば岩の上の子日の松もをいにけるかな

inishie no	In ancient times
tane to shi mireba	'Twas but a seed:
iwa no ue no	Upon the rocks
ne no hi no matsu mo	Rooted even a New Year pine[2]
oinikeru kana	Has aged, it seems.

4

On the last day of the Fourth Month, when at a mountain retreat with a group of courtiers to listen for cuckoos.[3]

都人待つほどしるくほとゝぎす月のこなたに今日は鳴かなむ

miyakobito	Capital folk
matsu hodo shiruku	Are simply waiting for you,
hototogisu	O, cuckoo:
tsuki no konata ni	This side of the month,
kyō wa nakanamu	Today, I would have you sing!

---

[1] This is believed to refer to the mountain retreat of Sanekata's uncle, Naritoki, the Koshirakawaden 小白川殿.
[2] A reference to the court ritual of gathering young pine at New Year, in order to pray for longevity.
[3] *Hototogisu* ('lesser cuckoo' (*Cuculus poliocephalus*)): this is a migratory bird which winters in India or southern China, and arrives in Japan around May, leaving again for warmer climes in September. The bird's song was admired – hence the outing mentioned here – and it was a source of poetic inspiration from the earliest times.

5

At a reading of the eight volumes of the Lotus Sutra to draw closer to the Buddha, held at the Shirakawa estate.

けふよりは露のいのちもおしからず蓮にうかぶ玉とちぎれば

kyō yori wa	From this day on
tsuyu no inochi mo	My dewdrop life
oshikarazu	I'll not regret: for
hachisu ni ukabu	Floating on the lotus is
tama to chigireba	A jewel, linked to me now…

6

When at a mountain retreat, on hearing the chirping of the evening cicadas.[1]

葉をしげみゝやまのかげやまがふらむあくるもしらぬひぐらしの聲

ha o shigemi	Do the leaves in such profusion in
miyama no kage ya	The mountains cast their shade
magauramu	that
akuru mo shiranu	Confused, perhaps, and
higurashi no koe	Unknowing of the dawn,
	The evening cicadas chirp on?

---

[1] *Higurashi* 蜩・茅蜩: commonly referred to in English as the 'evening cicada' or 'higurashi cicada', this insect (*Tanna japonensis*) is widely found throughout East Asia. It has a distinctive metallic cry, which it makes from the rainy season in early summer through to the autumn. The insect's name is homophonous with *higurashi* 日暮らし ('all day long') and also *hi kurashi* 日昏し ('(a) dark day' – and by association 'evening') and so it provided a fertile resource for wordplay.

7

When the sun went down, while aboard ship at Shikitsu.[1]

舟ながらこよひばかりは旅寝せむ敷津の波に夢はさむとも

fune nagara　　　　　　　　　　Aboard,
koyoi bakari wa　　　　　　　On just this night
tabinesemu　　　　　　　　　　Let's sleep;
shikitsu no nami ni　　　　Though the waves of Shikitsu
yume wa samu tomo　　　　　From our dreams awake us.

8

When the Kōshin rite[2] was celebrated at the Koichijō mansion[3] on the Fifth Day of the Fifth Month.[4]

やどの上に山ほとゝぎすきなくなり今日はあやめの根のみと思ふに

yado no ue ni　　　　　　　Above the house
yama hototogisu　　　　　　A mountain cuckoo
kinakunari　　　　　　　　　Has come to sing;
kyō wa ayame no　　　　　　On this day sweet flag
ne nomi to omou　　　　　　Roots, alone, would be there, I thought.

---

[1] Shikitsu 敷津 was the name given to the coastline to the south-west of the Sumiyoshi 住吉 Shrine in the province of Settsu 摂津 (currently Suminoe 住之江 ward in Osaka city). It was used as a *utamakura* in poetry, primarily as it could be used as a pivot word with *shiki* 敷き 'spread'. In the poem, while not being used explicitly as a *kakekotoba*, it evokes spreading out one's bedding, as well as the spreading waves.

[2] The Kōshin Rite was a periodic religious observance which required people to stay awake all night to ward off illness and ill-luck.

[3] The Koichijō 小一条 mansion was the home of Sanekata's uncle, Naritoki.

[4] A reference to the day of the Sweet Flag festival, when the plants were hung from the eaves of houses to ward off illness.

9

Composed when the Major Captain,[1] perhaps bearing some ill will against me for something[2] and not seeing me for a while, sent to me saying, 'Why not come over to the Shirakawa estate?'

白川にさそふ水だになかりせば心もゆかずおもはましやは

shirakawa ni	Had to Shirakawa
sasou mizu dani	Inviting waters
nakariseba	Not come,
kokoro mo yukazu	Suffering
omowamashi ya wa	Would have remained rooted in my heart.

---

[1] A reference to Sanekata's uncle, Naritoki. He held the position of Major Captain of the Right (*udaishō* 右大将) for thirteen years, between the 11th day of the Tenth Month, Jōgen 貞元 2 [24.11.977] and the 7th day of the First Month, Shōryaku 正暦 1 [5.2.990].

[2] Other sources suggest that the cause of Naritoki's ire was that Sanekata had been having a relationship with his daughter – his own cousin – and Naritoki disapproved.

10

When I was at the Horikawa Palace,[1] and Lady Koma no Myōbu[2] was behind a folding screen, a globeflower was tossed over it, and I realised that His Majesty[3] was there, too.

やへながらいろもかはらぬ山吹のこゝのへになど咲かずなりにし

yae nagara	Eightfold,
iro mo kawaranu	Your hues remain unchanged:
yamabuki no	O, globeflower,
kokonoe ni nado	But within nine folds[4]
sakazu narinishi	Have you bloomless become…?

11

His Majesty's Reply:

こゝのへにあらで八重さく山吹の言はぬ色をばしる人もなし

kokonoe ni	Within nine folds
arade yae saku	'Tis not, so my eightfold blooming
yamabuki no	Yellow globeflower's
iwanu iro o ba	Wordless hues[5]
shiru hito mo nashi	Are unknown to all.

---

[1] The residence of the then Empress, Teruko (Kōshi) 媓子 (947-979). It was located at the southern end of Nijō 二条 on the eastern side of the Horikawa 堀川 river.

[2] Koma no Myōbu 小馬の命婦 (dates unknown) was a lady-in waiting to Teruko (Kōshi) and a recognised poet in her own right.

[3] The Emperor at this time was En'yū 円融 (959-991; r. 969-984).

[4] A typically complicated piece of wordplay and allusion here: Sanekata first uses a standard description of globeflowers, yae 八重 'eightfold' and associates it with Lady Koma (iro mo kawaranu いろもかはらぬ 'Your hues remain unchanged' – that is to say, 'You are just as beautiful and alluring as ever'). He then builds on the imagery by introducing the term kokonoe 九重 'ninefold' to make an allusion to the imperial court (the imperial palace in China was said to have had ninefold gates and so 'ninefold' came to be used to allude to the court), and returns to the floral imagery for his final remark sakazu narinishi, literally 'it has become that you do not bloom' meaning 'Why are you not appearing at court, any longer?'. The headnote, of course, supplies the answer: she has been dallying with the Emperor.

[5] En'yū also indulges in some elaborate wordplay here, using the phrase iwanu iro 言はぬ色 (literally 'colours which do not speak'), which I've translated as 'wordless hues'. By association, this is a subtle reference to kuchinashi 梔子 iro: a yellowish-orange shade which globeflowers could be, given that kuchinashi could also be read as meaning kuchi nashi 'without a mouth'. The message in the poem is: 'We are not at court, so there's no one to spread rumours (unless you do it…)'

12

My Response:

衛士が居しひたきに見ゆる花なればこゝろのうちにいはで思ふかも

      eji ga ishi   The palace guards do stand
hitaki ni miyuru   Kindling flames: at the sight
    hana nareba   Of such a bloom
kokoro no uchi ni   Deep within my heart
iwade omou kamo   I felt a wordless longing.[1]

13

A Further poem from His Majesty:

みかきよりほかのひたきの花なればこゝろとゞめてをる人もなし

    mikaki yori   Within the palace walls
hoka no hitaki no   Some other kindled
    hana nareba   Bloom it was, so
kokoro todomete   With a halting heart
oru hito mo nashi   To pluck it was there no one![2]

---

[1] Opinions are divided about what Sanekata means here, but the consensus is that he's saying: 'I was fond of Lady Koma long before you were.'
[2] En'yū's response is blunt: 'If you wanted her, you should have done something about it then!'

14

At the residence of the Princess of the First Order,[1] there was a beautiful cherry tree by the quarters of the ladies-in waiting; thinking of a particular lady, I attached a spray to my poem:

植ゑて見る人のこゝろにくらぶれば遅くうつろふ花の色かな

uete miru	This is planted to gaze upon
hito no kokoro ni	My Lady's heart
kurabureba	In comparison
osoku utsurou	More slow to fade
hana no iro kana	Are the blossoms' hues!

15

She replied, with the blossom tied to her letter:

植ゑて見る人のこゝろにくらぶれば遅くうつろふ花の色かな

kage ni dani	Even to its shade
tachiyorigataki	Is it hard to draw near:
hana no iro o	Of the blossoms' hues
narashigao ni mo	What knowledge have you,
kurabekeru kana	To make comparisons?

---

[1] The Princess of the First Order was En'yū's elder sister, Princess Sukeko (Shishi) 資子 (955-1015).

16

And I responded:

立ち寄らむ事やはかたき春霞ならびの岡の花ならずとも

tachiyoramu	Drawing near:
koto ya wa kataki	Is it, indeed, so hard?
haru kasumi	For in the mists of spring
narabi no oka no	Side-by-side upon a hill[1]
hana narazu tomo	These blossoms, without a doubt, are not!

17

On receiving a stem of silver grass from that growing before the Hall of Cool Purity,[2] the Mistress of His Majesty's Breakfast[3] composed this poem and fastened it to it, saying, 'Who might have sent this?'

吹く風の心も知らで花すゝきそらに結べる人やたれぞも

fuku kaze no	Of the gusting wind's
kokoro mo shirade	Intentions, I know nothing;
hana susuki	Silver grass
sora ni musuberu	So idly entwined, but
hito ya tare zo mo	Who has done it?

---

[1] Sanekata actually refers to an *utamakura* in Yamashiro 山城 province, *narabi no oka* 双の岡 'Narabi Hill', which was located north-west of the capital and had long been a place for imperial hunting and pleasure excursions. It was used in poetry, however, principally because *narabi* also meant 'side-by-side' and so it was often used to imply that two people were, or had been close. The implication in Sanekata's poem, building upon his first one, is 'I don't care if it *is* hard to get close to you - I don't want to!'

[2] A reference to the Seiryōden 清涼殿, the building in the palace compound where the emperor had his personal quarters and carried out his daily life.

[3] *Naizen no myōbu* 内膳の命婦 which I have translated here as 'Mistress of His Majesty's Breakfast', was a title given to the lady-in-waiting in charge of overseeing the preparation and serving of the emperor's food. This holder of the office features in a number of poetic exchanges around this time, but no details of her actual identity remain known.

18

While the courtiers were wondering about who should reply, I happened to come along:

風のまに誰結びけむ花すゝき上葉の露もこゝろをくらし

<blockquote>

kaze no ma ni	In the space 'tween gusts of wind
tare musubikemu	Who, indeed, entwined
hana susuki	The silver grass;
uwaba no tsuyu mo	Dewfall on the upper leaves
kokoro okurashi	Suggests a constrained heart…

</blockquote>

19

Composed while worshipping the Gods, at the foot of Asahiyama.[1]

朝日山ふもとをかけて木錦襷あけくれ神を祈るべきかな

<blockquote>

asahiyama	From Asahiyama's peak
fumoto o kakete	Stretching to its foot, are
yūdasuki	Cords of mulberry cloth;[2]
akekure kami o	Day and night, unto the Gods
inorubeki kana	Should we pray…

</blockquote>

---

[1] Asahiyama 朝日山 was a mountain on the northern bank of the Uji 宇治 river, not far from the capital. As its name meant 'Mountain of the Morning Sun', it was frequently used as an *utamakura* for poems on sunlight or the morning sun itself.

[2] *Yūdasuki* 木錦襷 were cords made from mulberry bark which were used to bind up one's sleeves during sacred rites. In this poem, Sanekata's image of the cords stretching the length of the mountain, with its connotations of size, is meant to reinforce his urging to pray to the Gods in the final two lines.

20

On seeing scarlet leaves at the Sakurai ('Cherry Well') estate[1] in autumn.

秋風の吹くに散りかふもみぢばを花とやおもふ櫻井の里

aki kaze no   The autumn wind
fuku ni chirikau   Blows back and forth
momijiba o   Scarlet leaves:
hana to ya omou   How like blossom they do seem,
sakurai no sato   At the Cherry Well estate!

21

At Amanogawa.[2]

天河かよふ浮木にことゝはむ紅葉の橋はちるやちらずや

amanogawa   At Amanogawa
kayou ukigi ni   To the drifting, floating rafts
koto towamu   A question I would pose:
momiji no hashi wa   Has the bridge of scarlet leaves[3]
chiru ya chirazu ya   Scattered yet, or not?

---

[1] A number of different locations have been posited for *sakurai no sato* 櫻井の里, which I have translated here as 'Cherry Well estate', but there is, as yet, no consensus on where it actually was. It is most commonly used in poems with a spring theme because of the association of cherry blossom with that season, so Sanekata's use of it in an autumn poem is somewhat unusual.

[2] The Amanogawa River 天之川 was a tributary of the River Yodo 淀川, which flowed through the province of Kawachi 河内 (modern Hirakata 枚方 city in the north-east of Osaka prefecture). It was used as an *utamakura* as it was largely homophonous with *ama no kawa* 'the River of Heaven' (the Milky Way), which flowed through Plain of High Heaven (*takamagahara* 高天原), the realm of the gods.

[3] Sanekata is referring subtly to: Topic unknown. 天河紅葉をはしにわたせばやたなばたつめの秋をしもまつ *amanogawa / momiji o hashi ni / wataseba ya / tanabatatsume no / aki o shi mo matsu* 'Heaven's River, / On a bridge of scarlet leaves / Can you be crossed? / The Weaver Maid / Eagerly awaits the autumn.' Anonymous (KKS IV: 175). This poem suggests that the Weaver Maid makes her annual trip across the River of Heaven to meet the Herd Boy on a bridge formed of fallen autumn leaves.

22

When a group of us had gone to Uji,[1] Lord Kagemasa[2] wrote this on the lid of a cypress-wood lunch box and sent it over:

端姫に夜半のさむさもとふべきにさそはで過ぐるかり人やたれ

> *hashihime ni*
> *yowa no samusa mo*
> *toubeki ni*
> *sasowade suguru*
> *karibito ya tare*

> To the Damsel of the Bridge,[3]
> 'How fare you in the deep night's chill?'
> Should one enquire;
> Passing by without a word,
> Who might be this heartless hunter?

23

My reply:

はしひめに袖かたしかむほどもなしかりにとまらむ人にたぐひて

> *hashihime ni*
> *sodekata shikamu*
> *hodo mo nashi*
> *kari ni tomaramu*
> *hito ni taguite*

> To the Damsel of the Bridge
> Spread out a single sleeve
> There is no time at all, for
> With a man just passing
> Does she dally!

---

[1] Uji 宇治 was, and is, located a short distance south of the capital and was a popular location for aristocratic excursions. In later years it would become particularly associated with melancholy as the setting of the final chapters of *Genji monogatari* 源氏物語 ('Tale of Genji'), but that sense is absent from Kagemasa's playful poem here.

[2] Fujiwara no Kagemasa 景斉 (?-1023), was the third son of Fujiwara no Kuninori 国章 (919-985). Little is known of him beyond his parentage and that he held a number of provincial governorships in the course of his court career.

[3] *Hashihime* 橋姫, which I have translated here as 'the Damsel of the Bridge', was the deity who guarded the famous bridge across the river Uji.

24

In sorrow when former Emperor Kazan took holy orders.[1]

いひてなぞかひあるべくもあらなくに常なきよをも常になげかじ

iite nazo	To cry out loud
kai arubeku mo	Would there be a point?
aranaku ni	No, none, so
tsune naki yo o mo	For this impermanent world
tsune ni nagekazi	I'll show no sign of grief…

25

When Emperor En'yū[2] was transported to the cremation grounds.

むらさきの雲のかけてもおもひきや春のかすみにならむものとは

murasakino	At Gromwell Field[3] did
kumo no kakete mo	hyacinthine
omoiki ya	Clouds[4] cover all, yet
haru no kasumi ni	Did I wonder that
naramu mono to wa	To a springtime haze
	They would turn?

---

[1] Emperor Kazan 花山 (968-1008; r. 984-986) took holy orders in the Sixth Month, Kanna 寛和 2 [986], upon leaving the throne.

[2] Emperor En'yū 円融 (959-991; r. 969-984) died on twelfth day of the Second Month, Shōryaku 正暦 2 [1.3.991].

[3] Murasakino 紫野, which I have translated here as 'Gromwell Field', was a cremation ground in the northern part of the capital located near the Daitoku-ji 大徳寺 temple. Sanekata is using poetic license here, as En'yū was actually cremated in Nishiyama 西山 to the west of the city.

[4] Sanekata is playing with words in this poem, as *murasaki* 紫 'gromwell', also meant 'violet' and it was upon clouds of this colour that the blessed ascended to paradise.

26

Sent to Middle Captain Michinobu[1] with blossom attached, at about the same time:

墨染のころも憂き世の花盛りをり忘れても折りてけるかな

sumizome no	All are in ink-dyed[2]
koromo uki yo no	Clothes, yet in this cruel world
hanazakari	Blossom blooms most freely;
ori wasurete mo	Forgetful of the time,
oritekeru kana	Did I pluck these.

27

His reply:

飽かざりし花をや春の戀ひつらむありし昔を思ひ出てつゝ

akazarishi	Never sated of
hana o ya haru no	Blossom, does spring
koitsuramu	Yearn for them, I wonder;
arishi mukashi o	Times long past, that once were,
omoidetetsutsu	Keep coming to my mind.

---

[1] Fujiwara no Michinobu 藤原道信 (d.994) was one of Sanekata's colleagues and of the 36 Poetic Sages. His contemporaries esteemed his refined character, as well as his poetic talents, meaning he accumulated a respectable 49 poems in imperial anthologies.

[2] A reference to the dark clothes the court would have been wearing during the official period of mourning for En'yū's death.

28

At around the same time, at the Awata Palace:[1]

この春はいざ山里にすぐしてむ花の都はおるにつゆけし

<blockquote>

kono haru wa	This spring
iza yamazato ni	Why not dwelling in the mountains
sugushitemu	Should I pass my time?
hana no miyako wa	For in the capital, so like a bloom,
oru ni tsuyukeshi	All is drenched with dew.

</blockquote>

29

When remembering the reign of Emperor Kazan, together with Middle Captain Michinobu.

花の香に袖をつゆけみ小野山の山の上こそ思ひやらるれ

<blockquote>

hana no ka ni	The scent of blossoms has drawn
sode o tsuyukemi	The dew to drench my sleeves;
onoyama no	Onoyama:[2]
yama no ue ni koso	How strongly does the mountain's peak
omoiyararure	Attract my thoughts…

</blockquote>

---

[1] The Awata Palace 粟田殿, was a mountain retreat owned by Fujiwara no Michikane 藤原道兼 (961-995). The son of Fujiwara no Kane'ie 藤原兼家 (929-990), a man who achieved the positions of Regent, Chancellor and Prime Minister, Michikane's future seemed assured, but his life was cut short by illness.

[2] Onoyama 小野山 was located in the western foothills of Mount Hiei 比叡 and is used here as a euphemistic reference for the holy mountain itself. Kazan 花山, whose name literally means 'Flower Mountain', retired there after taking orders following his abdication.

30

Said to me by the same Middle Captain, on returning a pillow box which I had forgotten and left in the palace guardroom:

あくまでも見るべきものを玉くしげ浦島の子やいかゞ思はむ

aku made mo	Oh, how satisfying to open
mirubeki mono o	And look within this
tamakushige	Jewelled box, but
urashima no ko ya	The lad from Urashima,[1]
ikaga omowamu	What might he have thought?

31

My reply:

玉くしげなにいにしへの浦島にわれならひつゝをそく開けけん

tamakushige	A jewelled box!
nani inishie no	Why, in ancient
urashima ni	Urashima's
ware naraitsutsu	Imitation would I
osoku akeken	So foolishly open it?

32

His response, on departure:

おそくとも開くこそ憂けれ玉くしげあな恨めしの浦島の子や

osoku tomo	'Tis late and
aku koso ukere	To open it would bring only grief:
tamakushige	This jewelled box;
ana urameshi no	O, how regretful now
urashima no ko ya	Is the lad from Urashima.

---

[1] Michinobu is referring to the famous Japanese tale of Urashima Tarō 浦島太郎, who married the daughter of the Sea-Dragon King and spent time with her in king's palace beneath the sea. When he asked to pay a visit home, his wife gave him a jewelled box and strict instructions not to open it while on land. Of course, his curiosity gets the better of him and he does so, only to age to death in an instant. The tale had given rise to a superstition that opening a box belonging to someone else could bring bad luck and prevent friends from meeting again, so Michinobu is saying, 'I haven't opened the box, as I want to be able to see you again, my friend.'

33

Saying that I would come and collect some nightclothes I had left at Middle Captain Tsunefusa's[1] house:

返さむと思ひもかけじから衣われだに戀ふる折しなければ

kaesamu to	'I'll wear it inside out!'[2]
omoi mo kakeji	You've had no such thought for
karakoromo	My Cathay robe;
ware dani kouru	For a fond thought of me,
ori shi nakereba	You've not had for a moment!

---

[1] Minamoto no Tsunefusa 源経房 (968-1023) was the fourth son of Minamoto no Taka'akira 源高明 (914-982) and, like his father, was appointed to the position of Provisional Governor of the Dazaifu 太宰府 in Kyushu. Unlike his father, however, he died there and never returned to the capital. His talents as a poet were recognised by the inclusion of poems by him in *Shūishū* 拾遺集.

[2] Folklore had it that if you wore the nightclothes of a loved one inside out, you'd dream of them. Sanekata is saying, 'You don't care enough about me to wear my nightclothes inside out, so I may as well come and get them back.'

34

One autumn, when I invited Lord Michitsuna, the Middle Captain,[1] to go fishing, he said, 'You prefer taking life to the Way of the Buddha!', and I composed:

宇治川の網代の氷魚もこの秋はあみだ佛に寄るとこそ聞け

ujigawa no　　　　　　　　Upon the River Uji
ajiro no hio mo　　　　　　Sweetfish-fry against the nets
kono aki wa　　　　　　　　This autumn
amida hotoke ni　　　　　　To Amida Buddha[2]
yoru to koso kike　　　　　Are drawn, or so I hear!

35

His reply:

波の寄る宇治ならずとも西川のあみだにあらば魚もすくはん

nami no yoru　　　　　　　Though the wave-wracked
uji narazu tomo　　　　　　Uji it is not,
nishi kawa no　　　　　　　The Western River:[3]
amida ni araba　　　　　　 Were Amida but there
iwo mo sukuwan　　　　　　Would the fish be taken up!

---

[1] Fujiwara no Michitsuna 藤原道綱 (954-1020) was the second son of Fujiwara no Kane'ie 藤原兼家 (929-990) and a half-brother of Fujiwara no Michinaga 藤原道長. He held a variety of court positions in the course of his career, but is chiefly remembered now as a poet, his poems being selected for inclusion in the *Shūishū* and subsequent anthologies. His own fame, however, is eclipsed by that of his mother, who is the author of one of the major court diaries of the period, *Kagerō nikki* 蜻蛉日記, which documents her tempestuous relationship with Kane'ie. There are two translations of this work into English available by Edward Seidensticker Seidensticker EG (1964) *The Gossamer Years (Kagero Nikki) The Diary of a Noblewoman of Heian Japan*. Tokyo: Charles E. Tuttle Co. and Sonja Arntzen Arntzen S (1997) *The Kagerō Diary*. Ann Arbor: Center for Japanese Studies University of Michigan..

[2] Amida 阿弥陀 is the Japanised version of the Sanskrit Amitābha, and is the Buddha of Unlimited Salvation who pledged to save anyone who recited his name. Sanekata is implying that Amida will save the fish regardless of how they die, so it doesn't matter if they go fishing.

[3] Nishikawa 西川, which means 'west river' was another name given to the Katsura River to the west of the capital. Michitsuna is mentioning it in his poem, though, to create a resonance with the Western Paradise where Amida was believed to dwell.

36

When the Archbishop of the Ninna Temple[1] sent a selection of fruit to the Crown Prince,[2] I wrote this and attached it to the box it had been contained in:

思ふことなりもやするとうちむきてそなたざまにぞ禮し奉る

omou koto	Has all you wished
nari mo ya suru to	Come to fruition? So wondering I
uchimukite	Turn with zest to
sonatazama ni zo	You, your grace, and
raishitatematsuru	Make a humble bow.

37

His reply:

我ために無禮したまふことなくは思ふ心のならざらめやは

wa ga tame ni	If, for my sake,
muraishitamau	Such impertinence
koto naku wa	You committed not,
omou kokoro no	All your desires
narazarame ya wa	Would be fulfilled, would they not?

---

[1] The Archbishop of the Ninna Temple 仁和寺 was the Monk Kanchō 寛朝 (d. 998). He was the son of an Imperial Prince, Atsusane 敦実, and rose to high office in the clerical hierarchy on the back of these connections.

[2] In this case, probably Prince Okisada/Iyasada 居貞, the future Emperor Sanjō 三条 (976-1017; r. 1011-1016).

38

Composed at Kasuga.[1]

枝かはすかすがの野邊の姫小松いのる心は神ぞしるらむ

      eda kawasu   Branches intertwined,
kasuga no nobe no   On the field of Kasuga stand
   himekomatsu   White pines;
 inoru kokoro wa   My heart's plea
kami zo shiruramu   The Gods alone must know.

39

When snow fell and clung to the orange trees on the first day of the Third Month.

ときは春はなはさつきの花が香を鳥の聲にやけさはわくらむ

     toki wa haru   Spring is the season, and
hana wa satsuki no   The blossoms of the Fifth Month
   hana ga ka o   Bloom and give their scent;
 tori no koe ni ya   By the bird song alone
kesa wa wakuramu   Can I tell this morning.

---

[1] Kasuga 春日 was a wide area to the east of the ancient capital of Heijō-kyō 平城京 (modern Nara 奈良) surrounding Kasuga mountain. In the Heian period, the location was known as place for gathering the medicinal plants used to prepare health giving drinks for the New Year, and also as the location of Kasuga Grand Shrine 春日大社, the patron shrine of the Fujiwara clan.

40

In reply (by Middle Captain Michitsuna, or Michinobu)

ほとゝぎすなくべき枝と見ゆれどもまたるゝものはうぐひすの聲

hototogisu	Cuckoos
nakubeki eda to	From this branch should call
miyuredomo	Or so it seems, yet
mataruru mono wa	What we await is
uguisu no koe	A warbler's cry.[1]

41

Composed when the Kōshin Rite took place in the Ninth Month, during the period when Emperor Kazan was Crown Prince:[2]

もみぢ葉のいろどる露は九重にうつる月日やちかくなるらむ

momijiba no	Scarlet leaves have
irodoru tsuyu wa	Left a stain upon the dewdrops
kokonoe ni	and
utsuru tsukihi ya	Ninefold their hues will
chikakunaruramu	Shift:[3] that day
	Grows ever nearer.

---

[1] *Uguisu* 鶯 ('(Japanese) bush-warbler'; *Horornis diphone*): the bush warbler has its mating season in early spring, coinciding with the first blossom appearing on the trees, and so was regarded as a harbinger of the season.

[2] Emperor Kazan 花山 held the position of Crown Prince for sixteen years, from the 13th day of the Eighth Month, Anna 安和 2 [27.9.969] to the 27th day of the Eighth Month Eikan 永観 2 [14.9.984]. During this time the Kōshin Rite took place in the Ninth Month only in Eikan 永観 1, probably on the 8th day [16.10.983].

[3] A play on words, given that *kokonoe* 九重 'ninefold' was a euphemism for the Imperial Palace. Sanekata is saying, 'Soon will come the time when you will be emperor.'

42

Composed when various people were playing a poem rhyming game[1] in the courtiers' hall, and I was given 'footfalls':

秋の野にしめゆふはぎの露しげみたづねぞわぶるさを鹿のあと

aki no no ni	In the autumn fields
shime yū hagi no	The bush clover is garlanded with
tsuyu shigemi	Dew in such profusion, that
tazune zo waburu	Arduous, indeed, it is to trace
saoshika no ato	A stag's footfalls.

43

Composed for a painting of a woman becoming a nun while her parents slept.

つねならぬ世をみるだにもかなしきにゆめさめてのち思ひやるかな

tsunenaranu	This fleeting
yo o miru dani mo	World: even to see it is
kanashiki ni	Sadness;
yume samete nochi	On waking from their dreams
omoiyaru kana	How will they feel it?

---

[1] The game the courtiers were playing was derived from *tamuin* 探韻, a game where Chinese characters would be given out by lot, and the competitors would have to compose a poem with their assigned character controlling the rhyme scheme and ending the poem. In this case, they are composing poems in Japanese, and have to end their poems with their word or character they have been given. There is a brief account of a *tamuin* game at the beginning of the eighth chapter of *Genji monogatari* 源氏物語 ('The Tale of Genji'), *Hana no en* 花宴 ('The Festival of the Cherry Blossoms').

44

On the morning of the 8th day of the Seventh Month, after my son Kosogimi had died:[1]

たなばたの今朝のわかれにくらぶればなをこはまさる心ちこそすれ

tanabata no	The Weaver Maid
kesa no wakare ni	Makes her farewell this morning:[2]
kurabureba	In comparison
nao ko wa masaru	How much stronger
kokochi koso sure	Are my feelings.

---

[1] According to the commentators, the headnote to a poem which appears in a variant text of *Sanekata-shū* reads 'At about the time when there was a man who served in the Hall of Bright Speech known as the Lord Middle Captain who had lost his parents, he himself had to seal himself away in mourning'. The 'Lord Middle Captain who had lost his parents' is a reference to Sanekata, while the 'Hall of Bright Speech' (*sen'yōden* 宣耀殿) was the palace building occupied by Naritoki's daughter, Sukeko (Seishi) 娍子 (972-1025) when she entered court as a consort to Prince Okisada/Iyasada, the future emperor Sanjō. Sukeko entered court in 991, suggesting that Sanekata's poem was written at around that time Inukai Kiyoshi, Gotō Shōko and Hirano Yukiko (1994) Heian Shika Shū. *Shin Nihon Koten Bungaku Taikei*. Tokyo: Iwanami Shoten..

[2] The Weaver Maid and her lover the Herd Boy (the stars Altair and Vega) were permitted to meet only once a year on the night of the 7th day of the Seventh Month. Sanekata is saying that the Weaver Maid's grief this morning at having to say farewell to her lover for another year is as nothing compared to his grief at bidding his son farewell forever.

45

At around the same time, when I had seen my dead son in a tearful dream.

うたゝねのこのよの夢のはかなきにさめぬやがての現ともがな

utatane no	Dozing,
kono yo no yume no	My dreamworld was
hakanaki ni	Brief, indeed;
samenu yagate no	O, that ever wakeless
utsutsu to mogana	My reality could be…

46

After some time had passed, composed on the bridge at Nagara[1] on the way to Naniwa.

親も子もつひのわかれのかなしきはながらへゆけど忘れやはする

oya mo ko mo	For father and for son
tsui no wakare no	The final parting is
kanashiki wa	So sad;
nagarae yukedo	I live on and on, yet
wasure ya wa suru	Am I to forget it?

---

[1] The Bridge at Nagara (*nagara no hashi* 長柄の橋) was built across the lower reaches of the River Yodo 淀 in what would now be Osaka 大阪 in the Sixth Month of Kōnin 弘仁 3 [812] on the orders of Emperor Saga 嵯峨 (786-842; r. 809-823). It was washed away numerous times, often rebuilt, and came to be used as a poetic symbol of living on after the death of a loved one, as in this case. Eventually, however, the bridge fell into ruin and so later poets often composed about these, or the fact that there was no trace of the bridge remaining at all.

47

On-going somewhere with the Minor Controller of the Right[1] and seeing a cart loaded with brushwood going by:

春樵りの柴積み車牛よはみ誰がふるさとの垣根しめしぞ

haru kori no	Cut in springtime is
shibatsumiguruma	The brushwood – piled
ushi yowami	upon the cart with
ta ga furusato no	Such feeble oxen – o, cruel world -
kakine shimeshi zo	Whose house Has taken it for a fence?

48

At around the end of the Tenth Month, sent to Captain Nobukata[2] (or perhaps to a woman):

いつとなく時雨降りぬるたもとにはめづらしげなき神無月かな

itsu to naku	All unknowing,
shigure furinuru	Drizzle-drenched
tamoto ni wa	Sleeves
mezurashigenaki	Are not unusual at all
kaminazuki kana	In this Godless Month.[3]

---

[1] A reference to Fujiwara no Tametō 藤原為任 (?-1045), a son of Sanekata's uncle and guardian, Naritoki. He was made Minor Controller on the 11th day of the First Month, Chōtoku 長徳 1 [13.2.995] and promoted to Middle Controller in 999, so this poem must have been written between these dates.

[2] A reference to Minamoto no Nobukata 源宣方 (?-998): he was a son of Minamoto no Shigenobu 源重信 (922-995) and few details are known about his life. He entered court service in 982, and enjoyed a respectable career, rising gradually to the position of Middle Captain of the Inner Palace Guards, Right Division (右近衛中将 *ukonoe chūjō*) by 994, by which time he had also been promoted to Junior Fourth Rank, Upper Grade. He died of plague, presumably at a fairly young age, in 998. Sei shōnagon refers to him in *Makura no sōshi* as 'the Minamoto Middle Captain' in language which suggest they were on intimate terms, and a number of his contemporaries composed Lament poems following his death, suggesting he was well-liked by his peers.

[3] This was an alternative name for the Tenth Month, as it was believed that deities of Shintō all left their shrines for an annual conclave in Izumo 出雲 at this time, and so there was no point in praying to them.

49

On hearing this, the personage in the Hall's Shōnagon[1] composed:

大空のしぐるゝだにもかなしきにいかにながめてふる袂そは

ōzora no
shigururu dani mo
kanashiki ni
ika ni nagamete
furu tamoto so wa

Though the broad skies
Go so far as to drizzle
In their sorrow, yet
How should one gaze upon the long rains
Falling upon your sleeves, as the time goes by...

50

When Nobukata said he was going to serve at the Palace.[2]

いでたちて友待つほどの久しきはまさきのかづら散りやしぬらむ

idetachite
tomo matsu hodo no
hisashiki wa
masaki no kadura
chiri ya shinuramu

Setting off,
The wait to see you, my friend,
Will last so long:
The vines of yellow jasmine
May have lost their leaves...

51

My reply:

いそがずは散りもこそすれもみぢするまさきのかづら遅く來るとて

isogazu wa
chiri mo koso sure
momiji suru
masaki no kadura
osoku kuru tote

If all unhurried,
They will be lost?
In autumn colours
The yellow jasmine vines
Are difficult, indeed, to draw in!

---

[1] The identity of this person is unclear, although some scholars speculate that it is Sei shōnagon.
[2] The headnote to this poem actually reads 'When this person said they were going to serve at the palace', however, some texts of *Sanekata-shū* lack poem 49, and so the commentators suggest that in its absence, this is a reference to Nobukata, who is mentioned in the headnote to poem 48.

52

Written on the day of the festival after Captain Michinobu had been a dancer at the special festival and we had been there together, after we had both been promoted to the Fourth Rank.[1]

いにしへの山井の水に影みえてなをそのかみの袂こひしも

inishie no	In the ancient
yama'i no mizu ni	Indigo waters of a mountain spring
kage miete	Do I see your face;
nao sono kami no	Still are those long gone, god-touched,
tamoto koishi mo	Sleeves dear to me.

53

His reply:

いにしへの衣の色のなかりせば忘らるゝ身となりやしなまし

inishie no	Were those long-gone
koromo no iro no	Garments' hues
nakariseba	To be gone,
wasuraruru mi to	Would I forgettable
nari ya shinamashi	Become, do you think!

---

[1] Sanekata and Michinobu are thought to both have been dancers at a special festival (*rinjisai* 臨時祭), that is, one held not as part of the annual run of observances, but by special command of the emperor, in the Third Month, Kanna 寛和 3 [987]; they were also both promoted to Fourth Rank on the 25th day of the Third Month, Eien 永延 3 [3.5.989], so it seems likely that this poem was composed at a special festival held to mark the change of era name to Eiso 永祚, which took place on the 8th day of the Eighth Month of that year [10.9.989].

54

When Controller Tametō[1] had begun to cease visiting Nagayori's[2] house, at the turning of the year, His Majesty provided a strip of his own clothing as an offering for the Miyanome festival;[3] Tametō was visibly moved, so I composed:

あめに在す笠間の神のなかりせば古りにし仲をなに頼まゝし

ame ni masu　　　　　　Should the heaven-dwelling
kasama no kami no　　　　　God of Kasama
nakariseba　　　　　　　　Fail to come,
furinishi naka o　　　　To return things to what once they
nani tanomamashi　　　　　were:
　　　　　　　　　　　　How should I request it?

55

On returning from Usa, I sent this with some paper as a gift for a lady.

いさやまだ千ゞの社もしらねどもこやそなるらん少御神

isa ya mada　　　　　There are yet
chiji no yashiro mo　　A thousand, thousand shrines
shiranedomo　　　　　I know nothing of, yet
ko ya so naruran　　　From this one or that, I think, is
sukunami no kami　　　Sukunami no kami[4] – just a slip of paper!

---

[1] Fujiwara no Tametō 為任 (?-1045) was one of the sons of Fujiwara no Naritoki, Sanekata's uncle and adoptive father. He was appointed Minor Controller of the Right (*ushōben* 右少弁) on the 30th day of the Twelfth Month, Shōryaku 1 [18.1.991].

[2] Fujiwara no Nagayori 藤原長頼 (?-1010): the father-in-law of both Tametō and his brother Michitō 通任 (974-1039). This poem indicates a period when Tametō had been growing estranged from his wife and so had not been visiting her at Nagayori's house.

[3] The Miyanome Festival 宮咩祭 took place in the Twelfth and First Months in order to thank the gods for good luck in the past year and to pray to avoid misfortune in the coming one. It was sacred to six deities: Takamimusubi 高御魂, Ōmiyatsuhiko 大宮津彦, Ōmiyatsuhime 大宮津姫, Ōmiketsu no Mikoto 大御膳津命, Ōmiketsuhime 大御膳津姫 and Kasama 笠間 the Intercedor. This final deity was particularly called upon when relations between men and women were in need of repair. Hence, Sanekata's poem is a plea to Tametō to try and get back with his wife. The festival was carried out on the eastern side of the main hall of the palace, with various silken awnings hung between the pillars and three male and three female dolls woven of bamboo leaves, representing the deities, arranged on the veranda. Presumably, the Emperor's offering was used to dress one of them.

[4] Sukunami no Kami 少御神 is an abbreviated reference to Sukunabikona no Kami 少名毘古那神 who, together with Ōnamuchi 大穴牟遅, created the Central Land of the Reed Plains, or Japan, in early mythology. He is mentioned here purely for a play on words, in that *sukuna* means 'not much' and *kami* while meaning 'god' also means 'paper'.

56

Her reply:

廣前にまさぬ心のほどよりはおほなほみなる神とこそみれ

<blockquote>

hiromae ni	In the Presence
masanu kokoro no	You have not been, yet
hodo yori wa	The generosity, rather,
ōnaomi naru	Of Ōnaobi[1] – such a bounty of
kami to koso mire	Paper do I see!

</blockquote>

57

When we were at Uji, by the bridge floating upon the waters, we had been dozing and the sound of the river in the midnight moonlight was so beautiful that Captain Nobukata began:

うぢがはのなみの枕に夢さめて

<blockquote>

uji gawa no	At the River Uji
nami no makura ni	Pillowed by the waves
yume samite	And waking from a dream.

</blockquote>

And I concluded:

よるはしひめやいもねざるらむ

<blockquote>

yoru hashihime ya	At night the Lady of the Bridge
i mo nezaruramu	Must not sleep a wink!

</blockquote>

---

[1] The lady cleverly picks up on Sanekata's reference to a deity in his poem with one of her own. Ōnaobi no kami 大直毘神 was one of a number of deities born when the father of the gods, Izanagi, bathed in a river to purify himself after returning from the land of the dead. The deity's name means 'Great Rectification of Disorder', but the purpose of referring to it in the poem is because it contains the *ō* element, which means 'great', 'large', which is the opposite to the *sukuna* in Sanaekata's.

58

Seeing Captain Nobukata saddened, with his scarlet ties in disarray on the night of the New Rice Festival,[1] I began:

いかなるひものよはにとくらむ

ikanaru What is
himo no yowa ni The ice that at midnight
tokuramu Melts?

And he concluded:

あしひきのやまゐの水はさえながら

ashihiki no[2] *yama'i no* The leg-wearying mountain spring
mizu wa saenagara Waters are frozen, so…

---

[1] This is a reference to the *niinamesai* 新嘗祭, a festival celebrated at the palace every year on the last day of the Rabbit in the Eleventh month, to give thanks for the annual rice-harvest.
[2] A *makura kotoba* of unclear derivation, although one suggestion is 'leg paining' and another is 'trees like reeds'. It is used to modify *yama* 'mountain', *o* 'peak', etc.

59

One morning when snow was falling, the Master of the Left Capital Office, Lord
Michinaga,[1] was at the northern side of the Hall of Broad Beauty[2] and said:

あしのかみひざよりしものさゆるかな

ashi no kami　　　　　　　　From the top of my legs
hiza yori shimo no　　　　　To below my frosty knees
sayuru kana　　　　　　　　　I feel a chill!

I concluded:

こしのわたりに雪やふるらむ

koshi no watari ni　　　　　Down around the dell,[3]
yuki ya fururamu　　　　　　I wonder, might the snow be
　　　　　　　　　　　　　　　　　　falling?

---

[1] A reference to Fujiwara no Michinaga 藤原道長 (966-1027), who was later to become the *de facto* ruler of Japan through his marital connections to the Imperial house. He held the position of Master of the Left Capital Office 左京太夫 from 978-980, dating the poem to this period.

[2] The Hall of Broad Beauty (*kokiden* 弘徽殿) lay behind and to the north of the Emperor's quarters in the imperial palace and was one of the residences for Imperial consorts and empresses.

[3] Sanekata's original poem refers to a specific place, Koshi 越, which was mountainous and, therefore, well known for its snow. *Koshi*, however, also can mean 'hips' or 'backside', so Sanekata is poking fun at the young Michinaga's complaint about the cold.

60

At an archery competition, when snow had fallen upon the multi-coloured curtains, the Lay Priest Middle Counsellor[1] said:

まへかたのまだらまくなる雪みれば

      mae kata no　　　　　　　　The first team's
  madaramaku naru　　　　　　　　Motley curtain
      yuki mireba　　　　　Snow swept I see, and

I concluded:

しりゑの山ぞおもひやらるゝ

  shirie no yama zo　　　　The mountain for the second team
    omoiyararuru　　　　　　　Is in my thoughts.

---

[1] A reference to Fujiwara no Yoshichika 藤原義懐 (?-1008).

61

While waiting for the first cuckoo at the courtiers' hall:[1]

かき曇りなどか音せぬほとゝぎす

kakikumori Cloud-wracked, it is, and
nado ka oto senu Why sing you not a note,
hototogisu O, cuckoo?

Tamesuke[2] heard me and said:

鎌鞍山に道や惑へる

kamakurayama ni In the darkness of Mount
michi ya madoeru Kamakura[3]
 Have you lost your way?

---

[1] The *tenjō no ma* 殿上間, here translated as 'courtiers' hall', was a space on the south side of the Seiryōden 清涼殿, the palace building where the emperor lived and conducted business. Entry into the courtiers' hall was restricted to members of the nobility who had been granted the title of *tenjōbito* 殿上人 ('courtier'), meaning they were permitted to be in the presence of the emperor.

[2] Minamoto no Tamesuke 源為相 (dates unknown): a minor noble and friend of Sanekata.

[3] Mount Kamakura 鎌鞍山 was an alternative name for Yokawa 横川 on Mount Hiei. It is used here principally as it contains *kura* 'darkness', and so suggests why the cuckoo may have lost his way.

62

One night in the year before Tamesuke was due to receive his cap of rank,[1] on a night in the Eighth Month when the moon was shining brightly, I was talking to him and said:

数ふればいまいつゝきになりにけり

kazoureba	Counting up
ima itsutsuki ni	Now, five months
narinikeri	Is all you have to go!

He concluded:

むつきにならば訪ふ人もあらじ

mutsuki ni naraba	If this were the sixth,
tou hito mo araji	No one will enquire of me!

---

[1] 'Receiving a cap of rank' was a euphemism for gaining promotion to Junior Fifth Rank, Lower Grade, the ceremonies for which were carried out in the First Month. It is believed that Tamesuke gained his promotion in 990, dating this poem to the Eighth Month 989. Sanekata essentially says, 'You've only got five months to go until your promotion!' and Tamesuke replies, 'In six months no one will have to ask me about it!'

63

When I said, 'That's a pensive face you've got on there!' to a courtier who was gazing at the surface of the water in the drainage channel by the palace, he replied:

戀せまほしき影や見ゆらむ

    koisemahoshiki　　　　　　　　One longing for love,
    kage ya miyuramu　　　　　　　Is that the face you see?

I concluded:

八橋にあらぬ御溝のをちに居て

    yatsuhashi ni　　　　　　　　　The Yatsuhashi
    aranu mikawa no　　　　　　　Channel,[1] this is not, yet
    ochi ni ite　　　　　　　　　　On yonder side…

---

[1] The original poem contains a play on words, as well as a reference to another well-known poetic incident. The courtier is gazing into the imperial drainage channel, *mikawa* 御溝, close to the palace. Sanekata replies by mentioning the Eight Bridges (*yatsu hashi* 八橋) over the River Mikawa 三河 in the province which bore its name in the east of Japan. This was the site of a well-known incident involving Ariwara no Narihira which was recorded in both the 9th section of the *Ise Monogatari* 伊勢物語 and also in *Kokinshū*: Once, he was travelling to the Eastlands with one or two friends. On reaching a place called Yatsuhashi in the province of Mikawa, they saw there were irises (*kakitsubata*) blooming particularly beautifully by the river. Dismounting, and resting in the shade of a tree, he composed this poem, expressing the feelings of someone homesick, with the correct syllable of *kakitsubata* at the beginning of each line. 唐衣きつつなれにしつましあればはるばるきぬるたびをしぞ思 *karakoromo / kitsutsu narenishi / tsuma shi areba / harubaru kinuru / tabi o shi zo omou* 'A Chinese robe / I have worn so often I know it / As I do my wife; / Having come so far / This journey rests heavy on my thoughts.' Ariwara no Narihira 有原業平 (KKS IX: 410). In this poem, as well as producing an acrostic, Narihira subtly longs for the wife he has left behind in the capital. Sanekata is saying, 'You may not be as far away as Mikawa, but the one you long for is in the palace and so is equally unreachable.'

64

When passing in front of a certain dwelling on the day of the Great Purification Ceremony on the final day of the Sixth Month,[1] someone said:

小牡鹿の耳振り立てゝ神を聞け

saoshika no	Just as a stag
mimi furitatete	Pricks up his ears:
kami o kike	O, Gods, hear me!

I replied:

をむと犯せる罪はあらじな

omu to okaseru	My dear, a committed
tsumi wa araji na	Sin you have not one!

---

[1] This ceremony took place at the Suzaku Gate (*suzakumon* 朱雀門) to the imperial palace complex on the last day of the Sixth and Twelfth Months. This gate, one of fourteen, was located in the centre of the southern wall, and was the most prestigious entrance to the outer palace. For the ceremony (*ōharae* 大祓え) one hundred officials of the rank of imperial prince (*shinnō* 親王) and below, would gather at the gate and pray for the removal of sin and pollution from all the people of the state.

65

After having said he would not attend the dances, the Rokujō Minor Counselor[1] said, at the Gosechi Dancers' waiting area:

雲の上を月より先に出でつるは

>*kumo no ue o* Beyond the clouds lies
>*tsuki yori saki ni* The moon: before it
>*idetsuru wa* Shall I emerge.

I replied:

伏見の里に人や待つとて

>*fushimi no sato ni* Reposing at Fushimi is
>*hito ya matsu tote* A lady waiting - so say you!

---

[1] Exactly who Sanekata is referring to here is unclear, but the most likely candidate is thought to be Minamoto no Michikata 源道方, who was a Minor Counsellor between the 30th day of the Eighth Month, Shōryaku 正暦 1 [21.9.990] and the 23rd day of the Tenth Month, Chōtoku 長徳 4 [14.11.998]. His poem is somewhat pompous: containing a stock image for the palace *kumo no ue* 'above the clouds', and the reference to the moon. Sanekata does a fine job of bringing him down to earth by saying the real reason he wants to leave is to see a woman. He uses the place name Fushimi, as it is homophonous with *fushi mi* 'lie down (with) and see (a woman)'. 'Seeing' a woman was a standard euphemism for having sexual relations with her.

66

When the people of Lord Koichijō[1] were playing riddle games, someone said:

勝たず負けずの花の上の露

   katazu makezu no   Neither victor nor loser
   hana no ue no tsuyu   Dew upon the blossom is…

I replied:

すまひ草あはする人のなければや

   sumaigusa   While the sumo grass[2]
   awasuru hito no   By someone is
   nakereba ya   Untouched?

---

[1] A reference to Sanekata's uncle, Fujiwara no Naritoki.
[2] *Sumaigusa*, or 'sumo grass' is thought to be the old Japanese name for bindweed. Sanekata uses it here to build upon the reference to winning and losing in the first half of the poem.

67

When one of the ladies of the palace had taken my fan and not returned it:

誰がために惜しき扇のつまならん

    ta ga tame ni   For whose sake
    oshiki augi no   So heartlessly to my fan
    tsumanaran   Do you cling?

She replied:

取れかし虎の伏せる野邊かは

    torekashi tora no   Come and get it - am I a tigress
    fuseru nobe ka wa   Lying in her den?

68

Around the Eighth Month on a night when the moon was bright, Former Emperor Kazan said we should compose a poem in an incorrect format:[1]

秋の夜に山ほとゝぎす鳴かませば

    aki no yo ni   On an autumn night
    yama hototogisu   Should a mountain cuckoo
    nakamaseba   Burst into song?

I concluded:

垣根の月や花と見えまし

    kakine no tsuki ya   The moon upon fence
    hana to miemashi   Might seem as blossom.

---

[1] In other words, a poem where images or expressions conventionally associated with one season were used with another. In this case the *hototogisu*, or 'cuckoo', a summer bird, is associated with autumn.

69

On a day when the gentlemen from the Nijō Palace[1] were bestowing charitable gifts, seeing large number of large boxes, Tamesuke said:

かの櫃は何ぞの櫃ぞおぼつかな

kano hitsu wa	Yonder box:
nani zo no hitsu zo	What lies within,
obotu kana	I wonder?

I replied:

かたひの前のほかひなりけり

katai no mae no	Placed before the beggars'
hokai narikeri	Arms, their alms![2]

70

On Controller Tametō,[3] when he returned in the morning from an assignation.

たが里にいかにしのぶぞほとゝぎすをのが垣根は花や散りにし

ta ga sato ni	At whose dwelling
ika ni shinobu zo	Have you secretly been calling,
hototogisu	O, cuckoo?
ono ga kakine wa	Has your own fence
hana ya chirinishi	Lost all its blooms?

---

[1] At this time Fujiwara no Michitaka 藤原道隆, Fujiwara no Michikane 藤原道兼 and Fujiwara no Sanesuke 藤原実資 were all resident at Nijō, and it is unclear whether Sanekata is referring to one or all of them.

[2] The original poem contains a play on words between the cry, *hokai*, given by beggars looking for charity, and the special containers, *hokai* 外居, gifts were placed in.

[3] Fujiwara no Tametō 藤原為任 (?-1045), Sanekata's step-brother and cousin.

71

Composed when Middle Captain Michinobu [1] had remarked on how fleeting the world was, and then said he was going pheasant hunting the following day:

たつ雉のうはのそらなる心地にものがれがたきは世にこそありけれ

tatsu kiji no	As a starting pheasant
uwa no soranaru	In the heights of heaven
kokochi ni mo	Do you feel, yet
nogaregataki wa	Impossible to flee
yo ni koso arikere	Is this world of ours.

72

Composed at Former Emperor En'yū's Day of the Rat celebration:[2]

紫の雲のたなびく松なれば緑の色もことに見えけり

murasaki no	Violet,
kumo no tanabiku	The clouds stream
matsu nareba	Above the pines, so
midori no iro mo	Their shades of green are
koto ni miekeri	Indeed, most fine.

---

[1] A reference to Fujiwara no Michinobu 藤原道信 (d.994), one of Sanekata's colleagues and of the 36 Poetic Sages.

[2] En'yū's Day of the Rat celebration (*mi-ne no hi* 御子日) is known to have taken place at Murasakino 紫野 in the north of the capital on the 13th day of the Second Month, Kanna 寛和 1 [7.3.985]. This was rather late, as it usually took place in the First Month, and involved an aristocratic outing to gather pine seedlings and other fresh greens to brew medicines for health and longevity in the coming year. *Murasaki* literally means 'violet', hence Sanekata's reference to 'violet clouds' in his poem.

73

Composed when Controller Tametō said he was going pheasant hunting on hearing that his lady at Sanjō¹ had given birth to their first child.

きゞすゝむ小塩の原の小松原とりはじめたる千代のかずかも

kigisu sumu	Pheasant roosting
oshio no hara no	Oshio Fields'²
komatsubara	Pine saplings do but
toriwazimetaru	Begin to number
chiyo no kazu kamo	The one thousand generations of his years.

74

His reply:

小塩山しらざりつるをすむ鳥のとふにつけてもおどろかれぬる

oshio yama	Upon Oshio Hill
shirazaritsuru o	All unexpecting,
sumu tori no	A roosting bird
tou ni tsuketemo	Takes flight; your enquiry
odorokarenuru	Was startling, indeed!

---

[1] I have used a bit of license in the translation here, as the headnote actually says simply 'a child had been born at Sanjō'. The assumption is that the mother was Tametō's wife, in that it is unlikely that he would be going to obtain pheasants as a gift to the family if she were not, but it is impossible to be certain.

[2] Oshio Fields 小塩の原 were probably the foothills around Mount Oshio 小塩山 to the south-west of the capital which were well-known as a hunting ground in Heian times.

75

Composed at Emperor Kazan's poetry competition:[1]

のどかにも頼まるゝかなちりたゝぬ花の都の櫻とおもへば

> nodoka ni mo
> tanomaruru kana
> chiritatanu
> hana no miyako no
> sakura to omoeba

> O, for this peace and calm
> Is my only wish;
> Never to fall,
> Our flowered Capital's
> Cherry blossom it is, I feel.

76

Composed on the Moon, at the same poetry competition:

月かげをやどにしとむるものならば思はぬ山は思はざらまし

> tsukikage o
> yado ni shi tomuru
> mono naraba
> omowanu yama wa
> omowazaramashi

> The moonlight
> Within my room come to rest:
> Should it be so,
> Unthinking to the mountains[2] -
> I'll dismiss it from my thoughts!

---

[1] The poetry competition took place on the 10th day of the Sixth Month, Kanna 寛和 2 [19.7.986]. The 'peace and calm' Sanekata mentions is a reference to Kazan's reign, and the poem an indirect plea for him to continue in office.

[2] 'Going to the mountains' was a euphemism for taking holy orders and retiring from public life and, in fact, only thirteen days after presiding over this poetry competition, on the 23rd day of the Sixth Month, Kanna 2 [1.8.986], Kazan abdicated and took orders. Obviously, Sanekata was aware of the Emperor's plans, and the poem is an attempt to remind him of all the beauty in the world which he would have to give up once he became a priest.

77

Composed in the autumn, after the death of Middle Captain Michinobu,[1] who had promised to accompany me to view the blossoms in the Eighth Month.

見むといひし人はゝかなく消えにしをひとりつゆけき秋のはなかな

mimu to iishi	'Let's go!' said
hito wa hakanaku	He: here fleetingly and
kienishi o	Gone;
hitori tsuyukeki	Alone and dew-drenched is
aki no hana kana	A bloom in autumn.

78

Composed on hearing a stag, while at the Shirakawa estate:

憂き世には山のあなたのゆかしきに鹿のねながらいやはねらるゝ

uki yo ni wa	The world of sorrows lies
yama no anata no	Beyond yonder hill;
yukashiki ni	So full of longing is
shika no nenagara	The stag's cry,
iya wa neraruru	Will sleep ever find me?

---

[1] Michinobu died on 11th day of the Seventh Month, Shōryaku 正暦 5 [20.8.994], and the headnote is ambiguous as to whether Sanekata is recalling something that happened the following year, or regretting something which did not take place.

79

On hearing that someone using the name of Sanekata, Assistant Captain of the Middle Palace Guards,[1] had been visiting a certain lady in the Tenth Month, I sent her the following:

たれならむいかで野守に言とはむ標縄の外にてわが名借りけむ

tare naramu	Who might he be?
ikade nomori ni	Somehow, to the gamekeepers[2]
koto towamu	I would pose that question;
shime no hoka nite	For without the demesne
wa ga na karikemu	Has my name been reaped!

80

Drizzle.

秋はてゝかみのしぐれもふりぬらむわが片岡ももみぢしにけり

aki hatete	Autumn is done, and
kami no shigure mo	Upon the upper reaches drizzle
furinuramu	Must have fallen, for
wa ga kataoka mo	Here on my hillside
momiji shinikeri	The leaves have all turned scarlet.

---

[1] Sanekata held the office of Assistant Captain of the Middle Palace Guards (*hyōe no suke* 兵衛佐) from the 2nd day of the Second Month Tengen 天元 1 [17.8.978] until the 1st day of the Second Month Eikan 永観 2 [6.3.984], so the poem can be dated to some point during this period. Given that unrelated noble men and women had very little contact, it was entirely possible for a man to visit a woman claiming to be someone else and leave her none the wiser as to his true identity.

[2] The original poem refers specifically to officials known as *nomori* 野守 who were charged with guarding the boundaries of the imperial hunting grounds against intruders. In poetry they were frequently portrayed as unobservant and allowing an illicit 'hunter' in, so Sanekata is drawing on a long poetic tradition to reinforce his image of someone taking his name and using it to gain access to the lady.

81

When my relationship with the Lady Kojijū[1] was still a secret, someone let slip that he had seen what she looked like,[2] so I sent this to her via a messenger named Tatsuya.

あだ浪のたつや遅きとさわぐなりみしまの神はいかゞこたへむ

adanami no	Was it false waves
tatsu ya osoki to	Breaking that of late
sawagu nari	Have made such a noise?
mishima no kami wa	The God of Mishima (who sees all),
ikaga kotaemu	How would he respond, I wonder?[3]

82

A letter which I had sent to the same lady was shown by her to Lady Koma;[4] despite this I heard that she was spreading spurious gossip about me.

こまにやはまづ知らすべきまこも草まこととおもふ人もこそあれ

koma ni ya wa	A nag:[5] should she be
mazu shirasubeki	Informed early of one's
makomogusa	Wild oats?
makoto to omou	Her oath is sooth for
hito mo koso are	Some folk!

---

[1] Kojijū 小侍従, also known as Kojijū no myōbu 小侍従の命婦 (dates unknown), was a lady in the service of Fujiwara no Akiko (Senshi) 藤原詮子 (962-1002), one of the consorts of Emperor En'yū, and the mother of Emperor Ichijō.
[2] In other words, that he had had a sexual relationship with her.
[3] Sanekata's poem contains a number of wordplays: *nami no tatsu ya* ('Have waves broken?) also contains *tatsuya*, the name of the messenger Sanekata has used, but the 'waves' here are the rumours he has heard that Kojijū has been seeing another man. *Mishima no kami* ('the God of Mishima') is used as the place name Mishima contains *mishi* 見し ('have seen'), with 'seeing' a woman being a standard euphemism for having sexual relations with her. Essentially, he is saying 'Are the rumours (of your infidelity) true? What would someone who has seen (your sexual escapades) reply?' The implication clearly is that he believes the rumours to be true.
[4] See poem 10.
[5] The original poem contains a play-on-words on the word *koma*, which is the lady's 'name' and also means 'horse' or 'mount'. Sanekata then continues the horse metaphor, by referring euphemistically to his letter and its contents as *makomogusa* 真菰草 'wild rice', which was used as horse feed. In the translation, I've attempted to retain some of this wordplay, but with English language imagery.

83

When I had been secretly conversing with a certain party's daughter at the Koichijō mansion, the lady's mother got to hear of it and, being extraordinarily enraged, pinched her daughter most frightfully, or so I heard; around the evening of the third day of the Third Month, the personage from the Northern Hall[1] told me to 'eat the rice cakes'[2] and I composed:

三日の夜の餅も食はじわづらはし聞けばよどのはゝこつむなり

mika no yo no	Three nights of evening
mochi'i mo kuwaji	Rice-cakes: I will not eat,
wazurawashi	For, indeed, would I suffer,
kikeba yodono ni	Then, in the river meadows
haha ko tsumunari	Out picking cudweed![3]

---

[1] A reference to the principal wife of Sanekata's uncle and guardian, Fujiwara no Naritoki, and thus essentially Sanekata's stepmother. This lady's name is unknown, but she was a daughter of Minamoto no Nobumitsu 源延光 (927-976), and the mother of four of Naritoki's children.

[2] After a man had spent three consecutive nights with a woman, and consumed ceremonial rice cakes, they were considered to be officially married.

[3] Sanekata engages in wordplay to get his point across at the end of his poem: 'river meadows' (*yodono* 淀野) is homophonous with *yo dono* 夜殿 ('bedroom'), and *hahako* 母子 ('cudweed'; *Gnaphalium affine*) is homophonous with *haha ko* 母子 ('mother and child'), just as *tsumu* 摘む ('pluck', 'pick' (a plant)') can also mean 'pinch (someone)'. So, he is saying, 'I'll not marry the girl, because there's no doubt I'd suffer as her husband, if the mother treats her daughter so badly as to pinch her!'

84

At around the same time the Lady Shōjō[1] performed as one of the Gosechi[2] dancers and I sent this to her on her return:

神舞しをとめにいかで榊葉の變はらぬ色と知らせてしかな

    kamimaishi   As a goddess did you dance,
   otome ni ikade   O, maiden; somehow, that
    sakakiba no   As the sacred evergreens'
   kawaranu iro to Unchanging hues is my passion,
   shiraseteshi kana I would have you know.

85

When I was openly with the same lady in the northern hall, towards dawn we opened the shutters as the sky looked particularly fine; so, too, did my lady:

天の戸を我ためにとは鎖さねどもあやしくあかぬ心地のみして

    ama no to o   The portal of Heaven,[3]
   wa ga tame ni to wa For my sake was
    sasanedomo   Shut not, yet -
   ayashiku akanu How strange - endlessly for it to
   kokochi nomi shite open not
            Is all of my longing…

---

[1] The identity of this woman is unclear, although the term Sanekata attaches to her 'name', *omoto* 御許, and which I translate here as 'Lady', actually indicated a degree of intimacy and affection, and was used for ladies-in-waiting (*nyōbō* 女房) in aristocratic households and the palace.

[2] The *Gosechi* 五節 was a collective name for a sequence of five events conducted by the court in the course of the year. In order they were the New Year Festival (*ganjitsu no sechie* 元日節会) held on the 1st Day of the First Month; the White Horse Banquet (*aouma no sechie* 青馬節会・白馬節会 held on the 7th Day of the First Month; the Dance and Song Festival (*tōka no sechie* 踏歌節会) held between the 14th–16th Days of the First Month; the Sweet-Flag Festival (*tango no sechie* 端午の節会) held on the 5th Day of the Fifth Month; and Feast of New Grain (*toyo no akari no sechie* 豊明節会) held on the second day of the Dragon in the Eleventh Month. In this case, Lady Shōjō will have been participating in the Dance and Song Festival.

[3] A reference to the door of the Heavenly Rock Cave, into which the sun-goddess Amaterasu shut herself and so removed light from the world.

86

When the same lady once failed to appear, pretending to be away and saying she had gone to her estates, I went to the palace; the following morning the lady sent to me, saying:

天の戸をさしてこゝにと思ひせばあくるもまたず歸らましやは

ama no to o	If within the Gate of Heaven
sashite koko ni to	To peer from here
omoiseba	Had been your wish,
akuru mo matazu	Should you really have failed to
kaeramashi ya wa	bide 'til dawn
	And returned home?

87

I replied:

天の戸をあけてふことを忌みしまにとばかりまたぬ罪は罪かは

ama no to o	'The Gate of Heaven,
ake chō koto o	Open!' you say: such is
imishi ma ni	Best avoided; so
to bakari matanu	Failing to bide a while,
tsumi wa tsumi ka wa	Is it really such a sin?

88

When I heard that the same lady was suffering from an unpleasant illness and a doctor was performing some treatment or other:

いかなれば我しめし野と思へども春のはらをば人の燒くらむ

ika nareba	How has it come to pass?
ware shimeshi no to	Here are the bounds of my estate,
omoedomo	I thought, yet
haru no hara o ba	The springtime fields
hito no yakuramu	Have been set ablaze,[1] it seems.

---

[1] A reference to both the illness burning within the lady's body, and the moxa that the physician is probably burning upon her in an effort to effect a cure.

89

When I had returned home, after a particular lady had vowed, for some reason or other, that I should never visit her again, after some time had passed, lo and behold, she wanted me to go see her again:

なにせむに命をかけて誓ひけむいかばやと思ふおりもありけり

nani semu ni	And for what,
inochi o kakete	Upon your life
chikaikemu	Did you make that vow?
ikaba ya to omou	For you to live, and to see you more:
ori mo arikeri	Such times there were once…

90

To a woman, at the beginning:[1]

いかでかは思ひありとは知らすべきむろの八嶋のけぶりならでは

ika de ka wa	In some way or other
omoi ari to wa	Of my passion
shirasubeki	I should tell you;
muro no yashima no	For, in Muro, from Yashima Isle[3]
keburi narade wa[2]	Rising smoke it is not!

---

[1] *Ko'ōigimi-shū* 小大君集, another poetic collection, has the following to say about the composing of this poem: 'Middle Captain Sanekata composed this poem saying, "Why don't you say this to her?" when Lord Tametō was longing after a woman.'

[2] This is one of Sanekata's better known poems, as it was selected for inclusion in *Kin'yōshū* 金葉集, the fifth imperial poetry anthology as KYS VII: 378.

[3] Yashima 八島 was a well-known poetic location, where volcanic activity heated the water enough that it would evaporate and look like smoke.

91

This was composed when Minor Controller Tametō had taken this poem as his own:[1]

このごろはむろの八島も盗まれて思ひありともえこそ知らせね

kono goro wa	Recently,
muro no yashima mo	Yashima Isle in Muro
nusumarete	Was stolen from me;
omoi ari to mo	And of my passion I
e koso shirasene	Could not inform her!

92

To Saishō the Handmaid:[2]

たなばたに契るその夜は遠くともふみゝきといへかさゝぎの橋

tanabata ni	The seventh of the Seventh
chigiru sono yo wa	Month[3]
tōkutomo	Is the night for vows:
fumi miki to ie	Though it be yet far away,
kasasagi no hashi	Say you'll glance upon my letter and step
	Upon a bridge of magpie wings.[4]

---

[1] Again, *Ko'oigimi-shū* records more detail about this, saying, 'Saying how charming the poem (90) was, Lord Tametō sent it to a lady for whom he was yearning. A lady heard about this and laughed, then when passing by [Sanekata] said, "You have been saying recently that Yashima Isle in Muro has been stolen from you, so you can't use it to express your own love..." Sanekata then composes this poem to show her that despite having his original poem appropriated by Tametō, he can still use the same image to express his feelings for her.

[2] The identity of this lady remains unclear, although there is speculation that it could either be the same lady mentioned in the headnote to poem 175, or else the same Saishō who was one of Sei shōnagon's friends while she served at court and is often mentioned in *Makura no sōshi* 枕草子 ('The Pillow Book') – see Sei Shōnagon (2006) *The Pillow Book*. London: Penguin Books..

[3] The night of *Tanabata*, when the celestial lovers, the Weaver Maid and the Herb Boy (the stars Altair and Vega) were allowed their annual meeting.

[4] Legend had it that upon the night of the Seventh day of the Seventh Month, all the magpies of earth would fly up and form a bridge across the River of Heaven with their wings for the celestial lovers to cross.

93

Her reply:

たゞちにはたれかふみゝむ天の川うきゞにのれるよはかはるとも

tadachi ni wa	Hastening to
tare ka fumi mimu	Read a letter: who should do that, I wonder?
ama no kawa	For upon the River of Heaven,
ukigi ni noreru	Mounted on a drifting raft,
yo wa kawaru tomo	All may change in but a night…

94

When the Lord of the Koichijō mansion[1] sent a letter to Lady Suri,[2] she sent no reply, saying only that he should look for her in the Forest of Inaba (Rejection):

むすぶてふ山井の水もあるものをなにゝ因幡の峰をかくらむ

musubu chō	'From cupped hands,'[3] the poet says:
yama'i no mizu mo	Water from a mountain spring
aru mono o	We have aplenty, so
nani ni inaba no	Why upon Rejection's
mine o kakuramu	Peak should you be found?

---

[1] Fujiwara no Naritoki, Sanekata's uncle and adoptive father.
[2] The identity of this lady-in-waiting has not been established.
[3] A reference to: Composed on parting from someone with whom he had spoken by a rocky spring on the way through the Shiga mountains. むすぶてのしづくににごる山の井のあかでも人にわかれぬるかな *musubu te no / shizuku ni nigoru / yama no wi no / akade mo hito ni / wakarenuru kana* 'From cupped hands / Droplets cloud / The mountain spring – / It's not enough–as from you / Am I parted.' Tsurayuki 貫之 (KKS VIII: 404).

95

While at the same palace and hearing that a lady called the Palace Handmaid[1] had had her hair cut by a man.

よそにかく消えみ消えずみ淡雪の布留の社の神をしぞ思ふ

yoso ni kaku Far and far away,
kiemi kiezumi Melting and falling once more,
awayuki no A sprinkling of snowflakes,
furu no yashiro no Falls upon the shrine at Furu:[2]
kami o shi zo omou Whose god – your hair – is in my thoughts.

96

When a lady who served at the same palace, whom I had seen previously, became unapproachable after going to the Hall of Received Fragrance.[3]

わりなしや身は九重にありながらとへとは人のうらむべしやは

warinashi ya How unreasonable!
mi wa kokonoe ni Within the nine-fold gates
arinagara You may be, yet
toe to wa hito no Should my tenfold requests to visit
uramubeshi ya wa Cause such despite?

---

[1] The identity of this woman remains unknown, although there is some speculation that it may refer to the wife of Minamoto no Tomomoto 源奉職 and mother of Minamoto no Kinmoto 源公職 Inukai Kiyoshi, Gotō Shōko and Hirano Yukiko (1994) *Heian Shika Shū*. *Shin Nihon Koten Bungaku Taikei*. Tokyo: Iwanami Shoten..

[2] The shrine at Furu 布留 mentioned here is Isonokami 石上 shrine, which can still be found in Tenri 天理 about ten kilometres to the south of Nara 奈良. The shrine is one of the oldest in Japan, and was supposedly founded by Japan's legendary tenth emperor, Sujin 崇神. The location was frequently mentioned in poetry as the place name was homophonous with two verbs, *furu* 降る ('fall (of rain, etc.)') and *furu* 経る ('pass (of time)') and so was used to evoke these senses, as Sanekata does here.

[3] The 'Hall of Received Fragrance' (*jōkyōden* 承香殿) was one of the buildings in the Imperial Palace complex. The poem indicates that the lady in question has left the service of Sanekata's uncle, Naritoki, and taken up a position there, possibly in service to the consort of Emperor Kazan, Tadako (Shishi) 諟子 (?-1035). This has led her to break off her relationship with Sanekata.

97

Further, to a lady whom I disliked in such a way:

われながらわれならずこそいひなさめ人にもあらぬ人にとはれば

ware nagara	That I am now
ware narazu koso	Not as once I was:
iinasame	So shall I defend myself;
hito ni mo aranu	Lest by a lady who is not
hito ni towareba	Who she once was, I be charged!

98

Around the Third month, I went hawking in Ōhara,[1] and stopped on the way in a place where the cherry blossom was most beautiful; the following day I sent this to the Provisional Minor Captain.[2]

きゞすなく大原山の櫻花かりにはあらでしばし見しかな

kigisu naku	Pheasants cried
ōharayama no	In the Ōhara hills of
sakurabana	Cherry blossom;
kari ni wa arade	Abandoning my hunt,
shibashi mishi kana	I, for a while, was captivated.

---

[1] Ōhara 大原 lay to the west of the capital, and was well known as a hunting ground. It was also the location of Ōharano Shrine 大原野神社, which was often visited by emperors to pay their respects to the deity, Kasuga no kami 春日神.

[2] As indicated by the headnote of the following poem, this must be a reference to Fujiwara no Michitsuna, who held the post of Minor Captain from the 2nd day of the Second Month, Tengen 天元 6 [18.3.983] until the 15th day of the Tenth Month, Kanna 寛和 2 [19.11.986].

99

In reply, from Lord Michitsuna.

かりならでわれやゆかまし大原の山の櫻に鳥もこそたて

kari narade　　　　　Not for a hunt,
ware ya yukamashi　　Would I go, to
ōhara no　　　　　　Ōhara,
yama no sakura ni　　Where upon the cherry-covered hills
tori mo koso tate　　Even the birds do stand.

100

To a certain woman.

ものをだにいはまの水のつぶつぶといはゞやゆかむ思ふ心の

mono o dani　　　　　If only I could
iwama no mizu no　　Speak; then as water from betwixt the rocks
tsubutsubu to　　　　Gushing
iwaba ya yukamu　　Would my words go
omou kokoro no　　　With all the feelings of my heart.

101

And again.

おぼつかな我ことづけしほとゝぎすはやみの里をいかに鳴くらむ

obotsukana　　　　　Oh, how worrying!
ware kotozukeshi　　I sent my message
hototogisu　　　　　By cuckoo;
hayami no sato o　　How swiftly to the estate of Hayami,[1]
ika ni nakuramu　　　Has he gone calling?

---

[1] This location has not been satisfactorily identified, although a location on the north-west shore of Beppu 別府 bay in Kyushu has been suggested. Regardless of the location, it is used in the poem as it is homophonous with *haya mi* 速見 ('see swiftly').

102

The Governor of Mikawa[1] had said one winter that he wished to get hold of some thread, so the following spring I sent him some, and he replied:

去にし冬いとしも何に待たれけむ春くるものと思はましかば

inishi fuyu	Since last winter,
ito shimo nani ni	For my thread, O why
matarekemu	Should I have had to wait?
haru kuru mono to	That it would come with the spring,
omowamashikaba	I would have preferred to know…

103

When the Kōshin Rite was carried out upon the Seventh Day of the Seventh Month,[2] and the courtiers were composing poems.

たなばたの緒にぬくたまもわがごとや夜半にをきゐて衣かすらむ

tanabata no	For the Seventh Day of the Sever Month,
o ni nuku tama mo	Gems are strung on thread;
wa ga goto ya	One such as I,
yowa ni wokiite	Risen in the depths of night,
koromo kasuramu	Might have clothes sodden by su offering…

This poem is identical to *Sanekata-shū* 162, but is given here with a different headnote.

---

[1] There are various possible identities for the Governor in this poem, but it remains unclear exactly to whom Sanekata was referring.
[2] This reference dates the poem to the 7th day of the Seventh Month, Eikan 永観 1 [17.8.983].

104

When a number of nobles had gone to Kawashiri,[1] the Provisional Major Councillor[2] called for some entertainment from ladies who were other than maidens[3] and, when we were reciting poetry, I composed this on the topic of 'dreamlike feelings'.

行きやらで日も暮れぬべし舟のうちにかきはなれぬる人を戀ふとて

yukiyarade	We can proceed no further, and
hi mo kurenubeshi	Shall, no doubt, see the sunset
fune no uchi ni	From within this boat; while
kakihanarenuru	Rowing ever further away,
hito o kou tote	Goes the lady of my longing…

105

Sent to someone's house in the Tenth Month as a plea for some paper.

何をしてとよをかひめをいのらましゆふしでかたき神無月かな

nani o shite	O, what am I to do?
toyo'oka hime o	To Our Lady of the Fertile Hills[4]
inoramashi	I would pray; but
yū shidekataki	How hard to it is to string a mulberry gar
kaminazuki kana	In this Godless Month…[5]

---

[1] Kawashiri 川尻・河尻 was a name for the location of confluence of the Yodo 淀, Kizu 木津 and Katsura 桂 rivers to the south of the capital.

[2] This is thought to be a reference to Fujiwara no Michinaga.

[3] A euphemistic way of referring to prostitutes. It was common for prostitutes to frequent river spots which were the destination for aristocratic pleasure trips, and approach the nobles' boats in their own to ply their trade, so Sanekata's poem here can be interpreted as an expression of regret over the departure of his lover for a night. See Goodwin JR (2007) *Selling Songs and Smiles: The Sex Trade in Heian and Kamakura Japan*. Honolulu: University of Hawai'i Press. for a detailed account of the sex trade in Heian Japan and attitudes to it.

[4] The expression *toyooka hime* 豊岡姫 which I have translated here as 'Our Lady of the Fertile Hills', was an alternative way of referring to the Sun Goddess, Amaterasu Ōmikami 天照大神.

[5] Sanekata is using a familiar piece of wordplay here, in that *kami* could mean both 'God' and 'paper'. See poem 48 for 'Godless Month'.

106

Thinking of someone whom I had known since childhood.

ふたばより三嶋の松をむすばむと波うちいで〵えこそいはれね

futaba yori	Since 'twas a seedling
mishima no matsu o	Around yon oft glimpsed pine on
musubamu to	Mishima Isle
nami uchi'idete	Have I wanted to entwine; but
e koso iwarene	The rising waves
	Leave me bereft of words.

107

Recalling a lady whom I had forgotten, I paid a visit to her house and, as expected, was not admitted immediately:

わがごとや久米路の橋もなかたえて渡しわぶらむ葛城の神

wa ga goto ya	Is he as I, I wonder?
kumeji no hashi mo	The Bridge of Kumeji[1] simply
nakataete	Petering out and
watashiwaburamu	At a loss to cross it,
kuzuragi no kami	The God of Kazuragi.[2]

---

[1] The Bridge of Kumeji was a legendary stone structure famous, in fact, for not being a proper bridge at all and only going part-way. Hence it was frequently used in poetry as an image for a broken or suddenly terminated relationship between a man and a woman. The legend had it that the deity Kazuragi no kami 葛城神 (also known as Hitokotonushi no kami 一言主神) was commanded by the wizard En'nogyōja 役行者 to build a bridge linking the holy mountains of Kazuragi in Yamato and Kinbusen 金峰山 in Yoshino. The deity was embarrassed by his hideous appearance and so would only work during the hours of darkness, meaning that he was never able to finish the bridge.

[2] The God of Kazuragi, *kaduragi no kami* 葛城神 was an alternative name for the deity Hitokotonushi no kami 一言主神, the 'Master of the Single Word' who famously manifested himself to Emperor Yūryaku 雄略 on Mount Kazuragi. The legend goes that the Emperor and his party, dressed in blue with scarlet cords were ascending the mountain when they spied a party dressed in identical colours approaching them. After Yūryaku challenged the interlopers and had his men set arrows to their bows, Hitokotonushi revealed who he was, whereupon the Emperor apologised for his ignorance in wearing the same colours as the deity, and made an offering of his and his party's clothes to him. Hitokotonushi accepted the offering and graciously accompanied the Emperor to the foot of the mountain. Subsequently, however, he slandered the wizard En'nogyōja by accusing him of wanting to supplant the emperor. The wizard retaliated by binding him with a spell and commanding him to build the Bridge of Kumeji between Kazuragi and Kibusen. In later years, Hitokotonushi was often invoked for divinatory or oracular purposes, his responses invariably being in the form of a single word which could determine an individual's fate.

108

From a woman in a similar situation.

今はとて古巣をいづるうぐひすのあとみるからにねぞなかれける

ima wa tote　　　　　'No more, now!' I say;
furusu o izuru　　　　Gone from his accustomed nest is
uguisu no　　　　　　The warbler, and
ato miru kara ni　　　At the sight of his leavings
ne zo nakarekeru　　　I burst out crying.

109

My reply:

うぐひすの古巣といはば雁がねのかへるつらにや思ひなさまし

uguisu no　　　　　　A warbler's
furusu to iwaba　　　Accustomed nest, do you say?
kari ga ne no　　　　Of a goose[1] calling
kaeru tsura ni ya　　From his homeward flight
omoinasamashi　　　　I would have you think!

---

[1] The warbler was famous for abandoning its nests and building a new one each year, while geese faithfully returned from their migration to the same spot each year. Hence the warbler was a metaphor for infidelity, while the goose was one for faithfulness.

110

Sent to a woman whom it was impossible to meet with any longer without attracting public notice.

おほかたはたが名かおしき袖凍みて雪もとけず人に語らむ

ōkata wa	In general, would
ta ga na ka oshiki	Having such a name be so bad?
sode shimite	My sleeves are frozen, and
yuki mo tokezu	Should the snow thaw not,[1]
hito ni kataramu	Then would I speak of it!

111

Sent to the Lady Jijū,[2] when I had gone to the Biwa Mansion.[3]

おぼつかな夢路のをのゝたよりにやなをざりなりし宵の稲妻

obotsukana	Half-glimpsed,
yumeji no ono no	Can an axe upon a path of dreams
tayori ni ya	Connect us?
naozarinarishi	Twisted as
yoi no inazuma	A brief bolt of lightning in the night.[4]

---

[1] The snow is, of course, the woman. The implication of the poem is that the woman has broken off their relationship now that there is a chance of it attracting attention and is refusing to see him again. He is saying that he does not care about public notice, and warns her that he may reveal it himself if she does not relent.

[2] Jijū 侍従 was a lady-in-waiting at the Biwa mansion.

[3] The Biwa Mansion 枇杷殿 was the residence of Minamoto no Nobumitsu 源延光, who was the father-in-law of Sanekata's uncle and guardian, Naritoki. The *Eiga Monogatari* tells us that it was, in fact, Nobumitsu's wife who brought up and cared for both Sanekata, and the sons of Naritoki.

[4] This was a difficult poem to translate as the meaning of the phrase, *yumeji no ono no* 夢路のをのゝ, which translates as 'of an axe of the path of dreams' still eludes modern scholars. The remainder of the poem is also layered with word plays and double meanings: *yoi no inazuma* 'a lightning bolt at night' was a common image used to symbolise brevity and also reinforces the initial adjective *obotsukana* 'be unclear', 'be barely seen', while it is also preceded by the adjective *naoshi* which means both 'be straight' and 'be open (about one's feelings)', in a negative form and so meaning 'be crooked' or 'fail to be open'. Seeing someone in your dreams, on the *yumeji* 'the path of dreams' was thought to symbolise a romantic relationship. The general thrust of the poem then, would seem to be Sanekata saying that he has seen Jijū in his dreams, possibly implying that they have had a previous romantic encounter, but it was so brief he could not be frank about the depths of his feelings for her.

112

Her reply:

山人の斧のたよりとおもふともこりしもせじな峰の爪木を

>   *yamabito no*　　　　A woodcutter's
>   *ono no tayori to*　　　Axe has some connection –
>   *omou tomo*　　　　　Or so they think, yet
>   *korishimoseji na*　　　They will learn nothing from it:
>   *mine no tsumagi o*　　Kindling upon the peak.

113

Sent to a lady at the palace, attached to an ear of flowering miscanthus.[1]

これを見よ契らぬ野邊の尾花だにことこそいはね靡くものをな

>   *kore o miyo*　　　　Look on this well!
>   *chigiranu nobe no*　　Though it has made no pledge,
>   *obana dani*　　　　　even the field's
>   *koto koso iwane*　　　Miscanthus,
>   *nabiku mono o na*　　Wordlessly
>   　　　　　　　　　　Leans down…

114

And again, to a certain lady.

>   *omigoromo*　　　　　Festival-clad:
>   *mezurashigenaki*　　In the frequent
>   *harusame ni*　　　　Springtime rains,
>   *yama'i no ki mo*　　Trees by the indigo waters of a
>   *migiwa masarite*　　mountain spring, and
>   　　　　　　　　　The water's edge, grow ever larger.

---

[1] Miscanthus is an herbaceous grass which grows widely throughout Asia. It is poetically associated with autumn, and the rustling sounds the fronds made when brushed over by the wind.

115

To a woman with whom I had spoken, after we had parted for good.

ささがにのくものいがきの絶えしより來べき宵とも君は知らじな

sasagani no	A tiny crab,
kumo no igaki no	The spider, has her web
taeshi yori	Ceased to spin,[1] and so
kubeki yoi tomo	Though 'tis a night when I should
kimi wa shiraji na	come,
	You know nothing of it!

116

On returning from a certain place when it was late at night.

竹の葉に玉ぬく露にあらねどもまだ夜をこめて起きにけるかな

take no wa ni	Upon the bamboo leaves,
tama nuku tsuyu ni	Dewdrops, like threaded jewels
aranedomo	Are there none, yet
mada yo o komete	Still within the bounds of night
okinikeru kana	Have I arisen.

---

[1] Folklore had it that you could tell the approach of a lover by watching the spiders in your house start to spin their webs.

117

When I went to the same place on the first day of the Tenth Month, Middle Captain Michitsuna had been there since dawn; as expected, I saw him in summer clothes.[1]

身に近き名をたのむとも夏衣きのふ着かへてきたらましかば

mi ni chikaki	Light upon the skin
na o tanomu tomo	It is, 'tis said, yet
natsugoromo	Your summer garb
kinō kikaete	Had you but changed yesterday, and
kitaramashikaba	Come – O, how much better…

118

When the same lady had spoken to me through a sliding door, and I had said to open it, the lady stated that she had no means of locking it; my reply:

嶋の子は心ゆるさぬ天の戸はあくれどあけぬものにぞ有りける

shima no ko wa	For this island lad,[2]
kokoro yurusanu	The unrelenting
ama no to wa	Door to heaven,
akuredo akenu	Though dawn break, unopened
mono ni zo arikeru	Shall it be!

---

[1] The first day of the Tenth Month was the official day when courtiers changed from summer into winter costume. Michitsuna has been with the lady since the day before and so has not been able to change into appropriate attire. The implication of Sanekata's poem is that he is likely to be seen on his way home and thus everyone will know that he has been up to something.

[2] Sanekata is referring obliquely to the well-known tale of Urashima Tarō, who was given a jewelled comb-box by his wife, the daughter of the Dragon King, and told not to open it until he saw her again. Of course, he disobeys her and instantly turns into an old man. The lady has said to Sanekata, 'I can't lock the door,' implying that he may open it if he wishes. With his poem he says, 'I'll leave it closed all night, unless you are more definite.'

119

When there was no reply after I had sent a number of letters to the same lady.

みづかきのかきのみたゆる玉章は美濃のお山の松やいさむる

mizukaki no	From within the sacred walls
kaki nomi tayuru	Your writing has but ceased;
tamazusa wa	To such missives has
mino no oyama no	Mino mountain's
matsu ya isamuru	Pine[1] raised an objection?

120

At a time when the daughter of the Governor of Mino, still dependent on her father, had not replied to me.

おぼつかなかゝらぬたびもあるものを手向けの神の心盡しに

obotsukana	How concerned I am!
kakaranu tabi mo	On such a road
aru mono o	Did we never tread;
tamuke no kami no	With the journey's guardian god[2]
kokoro tsukushi ni	A source of worry.

---

[1] The lady's father has been identified as Minamoto no Mitsunaka 源満仲, the Governor of the province of Mino 美濃. Sanekata's poem asks, 'Have you stopped writing to me because your father objects?'

[2] A reference to the lady's father, who does not approve of their relationship.

121

The first thing I said to a lady.

かくとだにえやはいぶきのさしも草さしも知らじな燃ゆるおもひを

kaku to dani	Just how it is
e ya wa ibuki no	I cannot say, so of Mount Ibuki's[1]
sashimogusa	Plants aflame
sashi mo shiraji na	Do you know not a thing,
moyuru omoi o	Nor of the passion burning in me.

[2]

122

To the same lady, one morning as it was getting light when I had been by her shutters all night.[3]

あけがたき二見の浦に寄る波の袖のみぬれしおきつしま人

akegataki	Dawn comes unwillingly
futami no ura ni	To the Bay of Futami,[4] where
yoru nami no	The approaching waves
sode nomi nureshi	Have drenched the sleeves of
okitsushimabito	The offshore islanders.[5]

---

[1] Mount Ibuki 伊吹山 lay on the border of Ōmi 近江 and Mino 美濃 provinces to the north-east of the capital. The area was famous for moxa (*sashimogusa* さしもぐさ) production, and so the two are usually linked in poetry, as Sanekata does here.

[2] This is one of Sanekata's most famous poems, and was selected for inclusion in *Goshūishū* 後拾遺集, the fourth imperial poetry anthology (GSIS XI: 612).

[3] That is to say, the lady has not admitted him to her presence, and he has spent the night in frustration.

[4] *Futami no ura* 二見浦 ('Futami Bay'): confusingly, there are two locations with this name, both of which are used as *utamakura*. One of these is found on the inland sea coast, near to what is now Akashi 明石, while the other, now better known, is further east, on the coast to the east of Ise 伊勢. Both locations were known, and mentioned, in early *waka*, but the latter began to predominate from about the beginning of the twelfth century Kubota Jun and Baba Akiko (1999) Uta kotoba uta makura daijiten. In: Kubota Jun and Baba Akiko (eds) *Uta kotoba uta makura daijiten*. Tokyo: Kadokawa Shoten.. The commentators also indicate that Sanekata had this location in mind in his poem Inukai Kiyoshi, Gotō Shōko and Hirano Yukiko (1994) *Heian Shika Shū*. *Shin Nihon Koten Bungaku Taikei*. Tokyo: Iwanami Shoten..

[5] Sanekata uses an elaborate series of dual meanings and wordplays in his poem: *ake* is both *ake* 明け ('dawn') and also *ake* 開け ('open'). *Futami* is both the place name, but also *futa* 蓋 ('barrier') and *mi* 身 ('body', 'self'). *Ura* is *ura* 浦 ('bay'), but also evokes *ura(mi)* 恨み ('despite'). *Yoru* is both *yoru* 寄る ('draw near') and also *yoru* 夜 ('night'), while *oki* 沖 ('offing') also evokes *oki* 起き ('get up', 'awake'). To this is added the standard association of 'waves' being the tears shed by a frustrated lover. This means that an alternative translation for the poem would be: 'So difficult

123

When the courtiers had said they would await a cuckoo call and it had not done so by dawn.

待たずこそあるべかりければほとゝぎすねにねられでもあかしつるかな

matazu koso	Not to have waited, indeed,
arubekarikereba	That would have been better!
hototogisu	O, cuckoo,
ne ni neraredemo	Try we might, but unsleeping lay
akashitsuru kana	and
	Now the daybreak's come.

124

Topic unknown.

たなばたのこゝちこそすれあやめの草年にひとたびつまとみゆれば

tanabata no	Like the Weaver Maid
kokochi koso sure	It feels, I'm sure:
ayame no kusa	The sweet flag;
toshi ni hito tabi	But once a year
tsuma to miyureba	To be adorned![1]

---

to raise / Is the barrier around you, that in despair have I / Spent the night, tears / Simply soaking my sleeves, / On rising...'

[1] The original poem plays on the word *tsuma*, which means both 'spouse' (妻) and 'edge (of a roof)' (端). Sweet flags were hung from the eaves of houses once a year on the fifth day of the Fifth Month to ward off illness, so the poem says 'Sweet flags meet the edge (*tsuma*) of the roof once a year, just as the Weaver Maid only meets her husband (*tsuma*) once a year.'

125

When I arrived at that same veranda[1] and gave my usual knock, the lady, despite knowing it was me, had someone in ignorance of the state of affairs ask who was there most crudely; the following morning, the lady composed:

あけぬ夜の心地ながらにあけにしをあさくらとひし聲は聞きゝや

<pre>
     akenu yo no   Never would the night
  kokochi nagara ni   brighten,
     akenishi o   I felt, yet
    asakura toishi   Brighten up it did at last;
   koe wa kikiki ya   'Who's there?' asked
                       A voice - I wonder, can you
                              have heard it?
</pre>

126

My reply:

ひとりのみきのまろ殿にあらませば名のらでやみにかへらましやは

<pre>
     hitori nomi   All alone
   ki no marodono ni   Within your rough-hewn logs[2]
      aramaseba   Had you been,
   na norade yami ni   Without a word would I have halted and
    kaeramashi ya wa   in the darkness
                              Made my way home?
</pre>

---

[1] As in poem 122.
[2] Both the previous poem and this one contain references to a well-known *kagura* song: Asakura 朝倉. 朝倉や　木丸殿に　我が居れば　我が居れば　名のりをしつつ　行くはたれ *asakura ya / kimarodono ni / wa ga woreba / wa ga woreba / nanori o sitsutsu / yuku Fa tare* 'O, Asakura! / If within a hall of rough-hewn logs / I am, / If I rest there, / Announcing of his name and / Moving on – who's that?'

127

Around the Fourth Month, I heard movement from around this lady and, getting the feeling that she was not yet asleep:

まどろまぬ人もありける夏の夜に物思ふことはわれならねども

madoromanu	Sleepless
hito mo arikeru	A lady lies
natsu no yo ni	On this summer night;
mono'omou koto wa	The object of her pensive thoughts
ware naranedomo	Is not I, alas…

128

When I had not visited her for some time, after we had truly become close:

風吹かぬうらみやすらむうしろめたのどかに思ふ荻の葉の音

kaze fukanu	That no wind[1] has blown your way,
urami ya suramu	Do you resent it?
ushirometa	O, that does concern me!
nodoka ni omou	Simply recall
ogi no wa no oto	The sound of silver-grass leaves…[2]

---

[1] *Kaze* 風 'wind' was a standard euphemism for letters sent by a lover, so the poem starts, 'Are you upset that I haven't written in so long?'
[2] This was intended to recall the sound of the rustling of a lover's clothing.

129

At a time when was I confined as a result of many observances, and I found myself unable to keep calm for thinking of her:

もろともに起き伏し物を思ふともいざ常夏の露となりけむ

morotomo ni	Both
okifushi mono o	Awake and abed
omou tomo	Are you in my thoughts;
iza tokonatsu no	Look! Well-bedded pinks:
tsuyu to narikemu	Dewfall[1] upon them should we be!

130

I got a vow from a certain woman to love me even in the next world, but then afterwards, I wonder, what was it that happened?

誓ひてし事ぞともなく忘れなば人のうへさへ嘆くべきかな

chikaiteshi	To have vowed
koto zo tomonaku	Is of little moment,
wasurenaba	If you have forgotten;
hito no ue sae	Even on such a one as you,
nagekubeki kana	Shall sadness be bestowed!

131

When I had gone to the house of a lady who was closely watched by her mother, and she had felt it was inconvenient:

いはゞいへ親の飼ふ蠶も年をへてくる人あれどいとふものかは

iwaba ie	Tell her this then!
oya no kau ko mo	To your mother's tended silkworm
toshi o hete	At the appointed time
kuru hito aredo	Has come a spinner; yet,
itou mono ka wa	Is this a matter for regret?

---

[1] *Tokonatsu* 常夏 'pink' was frequently used for plays on words in poetry as it contained the word *toko* 床 'bed'. 'Dewfall upon the bed' could refer to the tears one wept for an absent lover, but in this context, being as '(close as two) dewdrops on a pink' meant 'to be married'.

132

Her reply:

繭ごもり親の飼ふ蠶のいとよはみくるも苦しきものと知らずや

mayugomori	Cocooned
oya no kau ko no	By her mother, a tended silkworm
ito yowami	Is weak, indeed;
kuru mo kurushiki	To have you come spinning is a
mono to shirazu ya	painful
	Thing - do you not know it?

133

Sent to a woman I had once been fond of, attached to a withered hollyhock.

いにしへのあふひと人はとがむともなをそのかみのことぞ忘れぬ

inishie no	Old, indeed,
aoi to hito wa	This hollyhock – as the day we met
togamu tomo	– you
nao sono kami no	Blame me, yet
koto zo wasurenu	Still, those times, so long ago
	I never will forget.

134

Her reply:

かれにけるあふひのみこそかなしけれあはれとも見ず賀茂の瑞垣

karenikeru	Withered
aui nomi koso	A hollyhock – and our love – yes,
kanashikere	It's sad;
aware tomo mizu	But, fondly of it I do not think:
kamo no mizugaki	Distant as the grounds of Kamo Shrine…[1]

---

[1] The original poem refers to the fence surrounding Kamo Shrine, but this implied the precincts behind it. A shrine fence, *mizugaki* 瑞垣, was a common metaphor for extreme distance in poetry, and the lady specifies Kamo here as hollyhocks were sacred to the deity of that shrine, and used extensively in its festival, in the middle of the Fourth Month.

135

When various members of the court had gone to a place in the mountains to listen to cuckoos, Minor Captain Kintō,[1] having feelings in a certain direction, intimated as much and, on returning, sent this the following morning:

山里にほのかたらひしほとゝぎす鳴く音聞きつと傳へざらめや

yamazato ni	Within that mountain retreat
hono kataraisi	Softly called
hototogisu	A cuckoo;
naku ne kikitu to	That you heard his cry,
tsutaezarame ya	Might you tell, I wonder?

136

When I was coming down from the capital as the messenger to the Usa Shrine, the Nijō Major Controller of the Left[2] said he was in strict seclusion and unable to meet me:

心うさのみやこながらもありけるを會はで別るゝたびと思へば

kokoro usa no	Heartlessness
miyako nagara mo	Within the capital
arikeru o	Does lie;
awade wakaruru	Parting, without meeting,
tabi to omoeba	On my journey - that's what I'll think!

---

[1] Fujiwara no Kintō 藤原公任 (966-1041) was already a gifted poet by the age of 19, when he was a regular participant in poetry competitions (*uta'awase*) arranged by the court. His poetic skills and knowledge were so valued by his contemporaries that he was often asked to be the judge of such competitions in later life. His crowning achievement was to be commissioned to compile the *Shūishū* on his own, the first single person to be given such a responsibility. Perhaps more important historically, however, is his collection of exemplary poems, the *Kingyokushū* 金玉集 (1007-11), the 'Collection of Gold and Jewels'. This provided a template for a substantial number of later works of poetic criticism.

[2] This position was held at the time by Fujiwara no Tamesuke 藤原為輔 (d. 986).

137

His reply:

別るとも別れもはてじ人心うさはしばしの事にやはあらぬ

>   wakaru tomo
>   wakare mo hateji
>   hito kokoro
>   usa wa shibashi no
>   koto ni ya wa aranu

> Though we may part
> This parting's not the end!
> Such heartlessness
> Has but a little while
> To last, has it not?

138

When I had returned from Usa, having pleaded for a comb from a lady at the palace:

來し道にけづるともなき旅人のたむけの神につくしはてゝき

>   koshi michi ni
>   kezuru tomo naki
>   tabibito no
>   tamuke no kami ni
>   tsukushi hateteki

> Homeward bound,
> With unkempt hair
> This traveller
> His offerings to the gods
> Has quite exhausted.

139

Her reply:[1]

かくしこそ隠しをきけれ旅人の露はらひけるつげの小櫛を

>   kakushi koso
>   kakushi wokikere
>   tabibito no
>   tsuyu haraikeru
>   tsuke no ogushi o

> So that's how you did it!
> Hiding it away,
> The traveller,
> Brushes off the dewdrops
> With a little boxwood comb.

---

[1] Other sources tell us that Sanekata pretended to have lost the lady's comb, and then presented her with better one he had obtained on his journey. Tsukushi 筑紫, where he had been, and which he mentions in the final line of his poem as it was homophonous with *tsukushi* 尽し ('be exhausted'), was famous for its combs, and so this was a natural present for him to bring back for her from his journey. The 'dewdrops' are the lady's tears at the thought that Sanekata has treated her gift – a love token – so carelessly.

140

When a woman I loved asked, 'Why didn't you see it?' about the dew upon the plantings before the Night Attendants' Offices[1] when I was leaving the Palace:[2]

起きてみば袖のみぬれていたづらに草葉の玉の数やまさらむ

okite miba	Had I arisen and gazed,
sode nomi nurete	Soaked, indeed would be my
itazura ni	sleeves;
kusaba no tama no	Would there be a point in
kazu ya masaramu	The gemlets upon the leaves Increasing, by so much, their numbers?

141

On seeing a spider spinning a web on the thread laid out on the Seventh Day of the Seventh Month,[3] Ko'ōigimi[4] composed:

織女のもろてにいそぐさゝがにのくもの衣は風や裁つらむ

tanabata no	The Weaver Maid
morote ni isogu	Keeps both hands busy;
sasagani no	A tiny crab,
kumo no koromo wa	The spider's garb of cloud
kaze ya tatsuramu	Might by a breeze be rent.

---

[1] The Night Attendants' Offices (*tonoidokoro* 宿直所) was where officials charged with guarding the palace and government buildings at night stayed when not out on patrol. Sanekata held the position of Middle Captain in the Inner Palace Guards, Left Division (*sakonoe chūjō* 左近衞中将) and so would have been their regularly, as the Inner Palace Guards (*konoe* 近衞) were responsible for guarding the inner palace, and both the national treasury (*ōkura* 大蔵) and that of the imperial family (*uchikura* 内蔵).

[2] That is to say, 'Why did you leave me so early in the morning that the dew had not yet fallen?' She is implying that he had left her with unseemly haste, and thus his feelings for her are not particularly deep. In his poem, Sanekata replies that had he stayed longer, it would have been so hard to part from her that he would have wept far more, and this would have detracted from the beauty of the dewdrops.

[3] It was customary to make offerings of thread and cloth to the Weaver Maid on the Seventh Day of the Seventh Month.

[4] Ko'ōigimi 小大君 (also Kodaigimi) was a lady-in-waiting to Emperor En'yū's Empress, Teruko (Kōshi) 媓子. She was on friendly terms and exchanged poems with a number of nobles and was sufficiently well regarded as a poet to have her work included in *Shūishū* and subsequent Imperial collections.

142

And I said in reply:

彦星の來べき宵とやさゝがにの蜘蛛のいがきもしるく見ゆらむ

hikoboshi no	That the Herd Boy
kubeki yoi to ya	Should come tonight,
sasagani no	A tiny crab,
kumo no igaki mo	The spider's web of cloud
shiruku miyuramu	Does clearly show.

143

A lady, to whom I had sent a cicada shell, wrapped in a lotus leaf:

いづれをかのどけきかたにたのまゝし蓮の露と空蟬の世と

izure o ka	On which
nodokeki kata ni	As something that endures
tanomamashi	Should I rely:
hachisu no tsuyu to	Dewdrops upon a lotus,[1] or
utsusemi no yo to	The cicada shell that is this world?

144

In reply:

蓮葉にうかぶ露こそたのまるゝれなに空蟬の世をなげくらむ

hachisuba ni	Upon the lotus leaf
ukabu tsuyu koso	Rests a dew drop:
tanomarure	Place your trust in that; so
nani utsusemi no	Why, for this cicada shell
yo o nagekuramu	World should you grieve?

---

[1] 'Dewdrops upon a lotus' was, of course, a reference to the teachings of the Buddha.

145

When I had sent a letter to a lady, and she had not replied, I tied a belt in a three-fold loop[1] and sent it to her

尋ばかり離りてまろと丸寝せむその総角のしるしありやと

hiro bakari	Just two hand's span
sakarite maro to	Apart, with me
marunesemu	Won't you, still clothed, lay
sono agemaki no	down?
shirushi ari ya to	A three-fold loop,
	Has this meaning, does it not?

146

When I had left a pillow at a lady's house, and then not visited her, she returned it, saying:

置きてみるかひもあらまし忘るゝをこれだに黄楊の枕なりせば

okite miru	Left, that you would see me
kai mo aramashi	Then might it have some use;
wasururu o	But that I am forgotten is
kore dani tsuge no	The only tale told by this boxwood
makura nariseba	Pillow.

---

[1] A three-fold loop (*agemaki musubi* 総角結び) was a particular method of tying *himo* belts that left loops to the left, right and above the knot, rather like a clover leaf. In his poem, though, Sanekata is referring to a well-known popular song (*saibara* 催馬楽) of the same title: あげまきや　ひろばかりや　離りて寝たれども　まろびあひけり　か寄りあひかり *agemaki ya / hiro bakari ya / agarite netaredomo / marobiaikeri / ka yoriaikeri* 'Hey, Agemaki! / Just two hand's span / Apart we slept, yet / We rolled together, / Or we came together!'

147

I replied:

かくなむと黄楊の枕にあらずともしらざらめやは戀の數をも

kaku namu to	That it is so is a
tsuge no makura ni	Tale my boxwood pillow
arazu tomo	Will not tell, nor
shirazarame ya wa	Can it know
koi no kazu o mo	The extent of my love for you.

148

To another, different, lady:

大堰川ゐせきのつゝむ水なれや今日暮れがたき嘆きをぞする

ōigawa	As Ōi River's[1]
iseki no tsutsumu	Dam-stopped
mizu nare ya	Waters am I to be?
kyō kuregataki	Today the sun is slow to set:
nageki o zo suru	A grief, indeed, to me.

149

After I had been seeing a certain lady's daughter in secret for a while, she died,[2] and feeling inconsolable I wrote to her mother:

契りありてまたはこの世にうまるとも面がはりして見もや忘れむ

chigiri arite	A bond we had, and
mata wa kono yo ni	Once more into this world
umaru tomo	Will she be born, yet
omogawarishite	With a different face
mi mo ya wasuremu	I may see and still forget her…

---

[1] The Ōi River 大堰川 flowed past the south-west foothills of Mount Ogura 小倉山 to the north-west of the capital, and was a frequent destination for aristocratic pleasure excursions.

[2] This poem appears in variant editions of Sanekata's collection with rather more detailed headnotes, which suggest that the lady died giving birth to Sanekata's child, and that the mother's response was to say she would never forgive him and send him the baby.

150

To the Lady Chūjō, at Sanjō.¹

みつとのみさはがぬ沼のけしきにもいつかとのみぞなをまたれける

<blockquote>

mitsu to nomi	'I saw it,' is all!
sawaganu numa no	A soundless marsh
keshiki ni mo	Do you seem to me;
itsuka to nomi zo	'Sometime' is the only word which I
nao matarekeru	As yet, await.

</blockquote>

151

When a certain lady wrapped up a cedar cone² and sent it to me.

たれぞこの三輪の山もと知らなくに心のすきのわれをたづぬる

<blockquote>

tare zo kono	Who it is that
miwa no yamamoto	From the foot of Miwa mountain³ -
shiranakuni	I know not - who, to this
kokoro no suki no	Hapless heart of
ware o tazunuru	Mine is calling.

</blockquote>

---

[1] The identity of this woman is unknown, but it seems likely that she was one of the women in service at Fujiwara no Naritoki's Sanjō mansion.

[2] The significance of such a gift or its purpose remains unclear, although one theory is that cedar cones were preserved to burn at the festivities for the Spring Equinox.

[3] Mount Miwa 三輪山 was a sacred mountain with a distinctive conical shape to the south-east of Nara. The mountain was poetically linked with cedar trees after the composition of: Topic unknown. 我が庵は三輪の山もと恋しくは訪らひ来ませ杉立てる門 *wa ga io wa / miwa no yama moto / koishiku wa / toburaikimase / sugi tateru kado* 'My hut is / At Mount Miwa's foot; / How I long / For you to come visiting / My gate where cedars stand.' Anonymous (KKS XVIII: 982), which is why Sanekata mentions the location in his poem here.

152

On seeing a woman I loved sleeping.

うき事にゆめのみさむるよの中にうらやましくもねられたるかな

      uki koto ni   A cruel thing it is that
yume nomi samuru   From a dream we must awake
   yo no naka ni   Within this world;
urayamashiku mo   How I envy her
neraretaru kana   The soundness of her sleep.

153

On seeing a certain lady destroying and disposing of the letters sent to her by a faithless former lover.

止めてだに今は見じとて嘆きつゝ誰が玉梓をいづちやるらむ

    tomete dani   Even those she kept,
ima wa mizi tote   'I'll look on them no more!' she says,
  nagekitsutsu
 ta ga tamazusa o   Grieving;
izuchi yaruramu   Whose jewelled missives, and
                                 Whither are they bound?

154

On hearing that a lady had begun conversing with another person,[1] despising a man who visited her only at lengthy intervals.

ほとゝぎす花橘の香をうとみことかたらふと聞くはまことか

     hototogisu   Does a cuckoo
hana tachibana no   The orange blossoms'
   ka o utomi   Scent disregard and
koto katarau to   Sing elsewhere?
kiku wa makoto ka   I've heard it but, can it be true?[2]

---

[1] The implication here is that the woman had started a new romantic and sexual relationship.
[2] A reference to: Topic unknown. さつきまつ花橘のかをかげば昔の人の袖のかぞする *satsuki matsu / hana tachibana no / ka o kageba / mukashi no hito no / sode no ka zo suru* 'Awaiting the Fifth Month

155

When a lady with whom I had become intimate in the Fourth Month, wanted it kept secret in the Fifth.

忍び音のころは過ぎにきほとゝぎすなにゝつけてか音をばなかまし

shinobine no	The first quiet call's
koro wa suginiki	Time is passed
hototogisu	O, cuckoo.
nani ni tsukete ka	And so for what
ne oba nakamashi	Might you raise a cry?

156

Although I knocked upon the gates of a place which I visited secretly, they were not opened so I returned home and, the following morning:

おぼつかなまだあけぬ夜の月を見てあまのとばかりながめられしか

obotsukana	How bothersome!
mada akenu yo no	As yet unlightened, this night's
tsuki o mite	Moon's traverse have I spent
ama no to bakari	Upon the Gates of Heaven
nagamerareshika	My gaze bending.

/ The orange blossoms' / Scent fills the air, and / Folk from long ago / With their perfumed sleeves come back to me.' Anonymous (KKS III: 139).

157

On hearing that Koben[1] had become intimate with another:

浦風になびきにけりな里の海人の焚く藻の煙心弱さは

ura kaze ni	In the bay breeze
nabikinikerina	Does stream,
sato no ama no	The Sato diver folk's[2]
taku mo no keburi	Kindled seaweed smoke;
kokoro yawasa wa	How like your fragile heart!

158

Bitter on hearing that the Empress' Lady Saishō[3] was spending all her time serving her mistress.

風早み嵐の山の紅葉ばもしもにはとまるものとこそ聞け

kaze hayami	The winds blow harsh
arashi no yama no	Upon the storm-swept mountain,
momijiba mo	so
shimo ni wa tomaru	Scarlet leaves, though
mono to koso kike	Below they stay,
	I've heard, do…

---

[1] The identity of this lady is uncertain, but it is most likely that she was a lady-in-waiting to Empress Sadako (Teishi) 定子 (977-1001).

[2] Sato 里 was a famous location in Awa 阿波 province, on the eastern coast of Shikoku. As a noun, *sato* meant 'village' or 'estate' and it carries that dual meaning here, too.

[3] The empress referred to here is probably Sadako. If so, this lady was the daughter of Fujiwara no Shigesuke 藤原重輔 and a friend to Sei shōnagon, who is often mentioned in *Makura no sōshi* 枕草子 ('The Pillow Book').

159

When a lady had taken my fan while I was at the Gosechi dancers waiting area,[1] saying she would return it on the day of the extraordinary Kamo Festival.

木綿かけて扇もいまは返してんまばゆく見えし日かげと思へば

yū kakete	Mulberry-cloth bound,
ōgi mo ima wa	Your fan, now
kaeshiten	Shall I return?
mabayuku mieshi	Blinding seems
hikage to omoeba	The sunlight, I feel.

160

My reply:

もろともに起くる朝もまだ見ぬになにの日かげのまばゆかるらん

morotomo ni	Together on
okuru ashita mo	Awaking, such a morning
mada minu ni	Have we yet to see, so
nani no hikage no	What sunlight could
mabayukaruran	Been so blinding?

---

[1] See poem 84. The Gosechi festival in this case would have been the Feast of New Grain (*toyo no akari no sechie* 豊明節会) held on the second day of the Dragon in the Eleventh Month. The extraordinary Kamo festival took place at the end of the Eleventh month, so the lady is saying she'll return his fan in a couple of weeks

161

Another woman's poem.

山人の斧の柄はみな朽ちにしをいかなる人のつま木こるらむ

yamabito no	The mountain man's
ono no e wa mina	Axe handle has completely
kuchinishi o	Rotted;[1]
ikanaru hito no	Who is it that might seek
tsumagi koruramu	To gather it for kindling?

162

On the Seventh Day of the Seventh Month, to the Lady Sako[2] in the Crown Prince's palace.

七夕の緒にぬく玉もわがごとや夜半におきゐて衣かすらん

tanabata no	For the Seventh Day of the Seventh Month,
o ni nuku tama mo	Gems are strung on thread;
wa ga goto ya	One such as I,
yowa ni oki'ite	Risen in the depths of night,
koromo kasuran	Might have clothes sodden by such an offering…

This poem is identical to poem 103, but is given here with a different headnote.

---

[1] The lady refers to the familiar folk tale of a woodcutter who came across two men playing a game of *go* in the mountains and, after watching them found that the handle of his axe had completely rotted away, and everyone he knew in his village had died long before. Essentially the lady is saying, 'Why would I want to rekindle a relationship which you ended long ago?'

[2] Lady Sakon (*sakon no kimi* 左近の君) is an alternative name for Ko'ōgimi, the composer of poem 141.

163

On hearing that a certain lady had been being visited by another man, I put on a show of ignorance and wrote this upon his fan[1] beside a drawing of Matsushima.[2]

まつにこそ思ひかゝるとききしまにねにあらはれて見ゆる藤なみ

matsu ni koso	On these pines, indeed,
omoikakaru to	Do you think fondly,
kikishi ma ni	I did hear;
ne ni arawarete	Their slumbering roots washed
miyuru fuji nami	Plainly by wisteria waves.[3]

164

When Tsutsugimi[4] was born, on the Seventh Night Middle Captain Michitsuna heard of it and started by saying to me:

知らずして七日ゆくまでなりにける數まさるなる濱のまさごを

shirazushite	All unknowing
nanuka yuku made	Upon the Seventh Night
narinikeru	Are we arrived;
kazu masarunaru	An age as great as
hama no masago o	Grains of sand upon the beach…

---

[1] The implication is that the man has left his fan behind at the lady's house, and that Sanekata has discovered it. The poem is a rebuke to her for being so careless as to make it obvious what has been going on.

[2] Matsushima 松島 bay was a beauty spot located in Michinoku 陸奥 province on the north east coast of Japan, which was famous for its many islets covered with pine trees (*matsu* 松).

[3] Sanekata's poem contains a number of puns and allusions: the lady is the pine tree (for whom the unknown man in pining), her roots (*ne* 根) are homophonous with *ne* 寝 ('sleep(together)'), while the wisteria (*fuji* 藤) is a sly reference to the man, who would seem to be a member of the Fujiwara 藤原 ('Wisteria grove') clan. The image of the 'wisteria waves' washing the pine tree's roots is an unsubtle suggestion of the man and the woman coming together physically.

[4] Sanekata's son, who seems to have been born a few years before his father's departure for Michinoku. Sanekata had seven children, and Tsutsugimi has been tentatively identified as a son who took orders under the name of Kenjin 賢尋 and eventually died in 1055. The unspoken end to the poem is that he will live as many years as there are grains of sand on the beach.

165

My reply:

これやこの海士の住むてふ濱びさし七日ゆくまのなにこそありけれ

kore ya kono	Well now, well now!
ama no sumu chō	Fisher folk dwell in
hamabisashi	Huts upon the beach;
nanuka yuku ma no	For this Seventh Night
na ni koso arikere	Fish is provided![1]

166

When Retired Emperor Kazan paid a visit to Kumano,[2] I accompanied him as far as the province of Tsu and one evening, on seeing many fisher-folk on the shoreline:

夕なぎに磯菜刈りにと急ぎつるあまのあまたも見ゆるうらかな

yūnagi ni	In the calm before the evening's sea-
isona kari ni to	breeze,
isogitsuru	Gathering seaweed,
ama no amata mo	Flurry
miyuru ura kana	A school of fisher-folk:
	Plain to see upon this shore…

---

[1] This is an obscure reference to Michitsuna's poem, but the assumption is that he accompanied his poem with a gift of fish for the occasion.
[2] Kazan visited Kumano towards the end of 991, or early in 992.

167

One spring, when there had been many fires in the houses of people in the world, a woman sent me a yam:[1]

この春はめづらしげなき焼けどころつれなき人はいかゞ見るらむ

kono haru wa	This spring
mezurashigenaki	Not uncommon are
yakedokoro	Roast yams and burnt out homes:
tsurenaki hito wa	A heartless man,
ikaga miruramu	What might he think of them?

167

In reply, I sent this to the lady who was burning:

煙たつひのもとながらゆゝしさにこはもろこしのところとぞ見る

keburi tatsu	Smoke rising
hi no moto nagara	From a source of flame[2] is
yuyushisa ni	Fearful, indeed, yet
ko wa morokoshi no	Far Cathay is this
tokoro to zo miru	Yam's source, I think.

---

[1] The lady puns in her poem, as the word for 'yam', *tokoro* 野老, is homophonous with the word for 'place'. As well as referring to the fires afflicting the city that year, she, of course, also implies that their relationship has become a burnt-out shell.

[2] Sanekata continues the word play in his flippant reply, as *hi no moto*, 'source of flame' could also mean 'source of the sun' – in other words, Japan – allowing him to bring in the reference to Cathay, *morokoshi*.

169

When I had begged some purple dye from the Director of the Bureau of Palace Equipment and Upkeep,[1] to say she would send it:

かこつべき故もなき身に武蔵野のわか紫をなにゝめすらむ

kakotsubeki	A complaint of
yue mo naki mi ni	A relationship with me have you
musashino no	none, so why
wakamurasaki o	Musashi plain's[2]
nani ni mesuramu	Fresh violet
	Might you request?[3]

170

My reply:

下にのみ嘆くをしらで紫のねずりの衣むつましき故

shita ni nomi	Within me all
nageku o shirade	Is grief, yet you know it not;
murasaki no	Violet
nezuri no koromo	Dyed clothes
mutsumashiki yue	Are most apt – that's why!

---

[1] *Tonomoryō* 主殿寮: this palace office was in charge of the equipment used during court functions, as well as more prosaic supplies such as oil and kindling. As this poem is not dated, the person Sanekata is referring to here cannot be identified.

[2] Musashino 武蔵野 ('Musashi Plain') referred to an area to the west of what is now Tokyo. The location was linked poetically with a number of plants which grew there, most commonly the gromwell (*Lithospermum erythrorhizon*) – see below.

[3] The lady's poem relies upon two well-known prior poems for its effect: Topic unknown. 紫のひともとゆへに武蔵野の草はみながらあはれとぞ見る *murasaki no / hito moto yue ni / musashino no / kusa wa minagara / aware to zo miru* 'A gromwell's / Single stem is reason enough: / Musashi Plain's / Grasses, all are / Dear to me, indeed.' Anonymous (KKS XVII: 867) and: 知らねども武蔵といへばかこたれぬよしやそこそは紫のゆゑ *shiranedomo / musashi to ieba / kakotarenu / yoshi ya so koso wa / murasaki no yue* 'All unknowing am I, yet / Mention Musashi Plain and / Long have I complained; / The reason? That, alone, / Lies with the gromwell.' (*Kokin Rokujō* V: 3507). The gromwell, *murasaki* 紫, was the source of violet dye, as well as being a standard poetic euphemism for a young woman desired by the poet.

171

Again, to a lady on some occasion or other.

むらさきの色にいでける花をみて人は忍ぶと露ぞつげゝる

murasaki no	In violet
iro ni idekeru	Hues emerging is
hana o mite	A flower glimpsed;
hito wa shinobu to	What a man would conceal is
tsuyu zo tsugekeru	Revealed in dewdrops.

172

Her reply:

白露のむすぶばかりの花をみてこはたがゝこつむらさきのゆへ

shiratsuy no	Silven dewdrop
musubu bakari no	Strung
hana o mite	Flowers glimpsed;
kowata ga kakotu	Who, then, would pretend
murasaki no yue	They're violet?

173

A poem for one of the Gosechi Dancers,[1] when she had spoken to me.

おぼつかないかにわれせむすべらぎの豊の明りのいづこともなく

obotsukana	How tantalising!
ika ni ware semu	What am I to do?
suberagi no	Amidst His Majesty's
toyo no akari no	Abundance of good cheer,[2]
izu koto mo naku	You are gone; who knows where?

---

[1] These were girls from good families, chosen to dance at court ceremonies. The custom was believed to originate with Emperor Tenmu 天武 (?-686; r. 673-686), who was said to have seen heavenly maidens dancing.

[2] In his original poem, Sanekata uses the term *toyo no akari* 豊の明り as a reference to the Feast of New Grain (*toyo no akari no sechie* 豊明節会), but the expression literally means 'an abundance of light', and was used to refer to imperial drinking parties. The commentators agree that the 'light' in the expression refers to the flush appearing on people's faces when drunk, hence my translation.

174

Her reply:

日影さす豊の明りにみしかども神代のことはゝやわすれにき

hikage sasu　　　　　　In the streaming sunlight of
toyo no akari ni　　　　　　A palace party did
mishikadomo　　　　　　I see you, yet
kamiyo no koto wa　　　　　　Such ancient matters
haya wasureniki　　　　　　Did I forget long, long ago.

175

When Lady Saishō, from the Hall of Bright Proclamations,[1] presented me with a pear.

かくれなき身とはしるしる山梨の麻生の浦まで思ひやるかな

kakurenaki　　　　　　Without concealment
mi to wa shirushiru　　　　　　Is this fruit – that I know well; but
yamanashi no　　　　　　To pears from
ou no ura made　　　　　　The bay at Ou[2]
omoiyaru kana　　　　　　Wander my longing thoughts…

---

[1] The Hall of Bright Proclamations (*sen'yōden* 宣耀殿), was one of the buildings in the palace compound, and was one of the buildings holding the living quarters of various imperial consorts. Saishō was apparently a lady-in-waiting there.

[2] The bay at Ou (*ou no ura* 生浦) was an *utamakura* in Ise 伊勢 province. It became known following the inclusion in *Kokinshū* of: An Ise poem. をふのうらにかたえさしおほひなるなしのなりもならずもねてかたらはむ *ou no ura ni / katae sashioi / naru nashi no / nari mo narazu mo / nete katarawamu* 'In the bay at Ou / Stretches forth a single branch / Of fruiting pear: / Shall we or shan't we – / Let's sleep together, and talk on it more!' (KKS XX: 1099). The actual location of this bay, however, has not been satisfactorily identified Kubota Jun and Baba Akiko (1999) Uta kotoba uta makura daijiten. In: Kubota Jun and Baba Akiko (eds) *Uta kotoba uta makura daijiten.* Tokyo: Kadokawa Shoten..

176

On seeing the serving girls Seki (Barrier) and Kokonoe (Ninefold), by the doorways of the same palace, conversing with a lady.

九重は關のこなたにあるものを關のあなたの九重やなぞ

kokonoe wa	Ninefold, the palace
seki no konata ni	This side of the barrier[1]
aru mono o	Does lie, so
seki no anata no	Beyond Barrier
kokonoe ya nazo	Why should Ninefold be?

177

Composed because Middle Captain Michinobu had slept with Seki at the Shirakawa estate:[2]

いかでかは人のかよはむかくばかり水もゝらさぬ白河の關

ika de ka wa	How is it that
hito no kayowamu	A man gains entry, I wonder?
kaku bakari	When not even
mizu mo morasanu	Water leaks through
shirakawa no seki	The barrier of Shirakawa.[3]

---

[1] As we have seen in previous poems in Sanekata's collection, 'ninefold' (*kokonoe* 九重) was a common image associated with the imperial palace. The 'barrier' (*seki* 關) in this case was the customs barrier at Meeting Hill (*ausaka* 逢坂), which controlled entry to the capital, and was frequently used in poetry as a metaphor for separation from a lover. Sanekata is engaging in wordplay given that the servant girls' names are the homophonous Seki and Kokonoe.

[2] Probably a reference to the mountain retreat of Sanekata's adoptive father, Naritoki.

[3] The Barrier of Shirakawa (*shirakawa no seki* 白河の關) was the customs barrier at the entrance to the northern region of Michinoku 陸奥, and frequently used in poetry as it contained the word *shira* 白 'white'. In this case, however, Sanekata is referring to the reputed vigour with which the officials at the barrier manned it, making sure nothing unauthorised got in or out of the province.

178

When I was sleeping with the same Captain, he said, 'This is most lonely and tedious! Let's see if there are any ladies around!' and sent off a servant who, on returning, said, 'There is only the voice of a lady saying "Oh, how my belly hurts!"'

園原やいかにやましく思ふぞも伏屋といはむこゝろやはなき

sonohara ya	In Sonohara[1] (your belly):
ika ni yamashiku	How painful
omou zo mo	Do you feel it is?
fuseya to iwamu	Of Fuseya (sleeping with me),
kokoro ya wa naki	Don't you think at all?

179

On hearing the sound of a cicada at dawn at a mountain retreat.

ほのぼのにひぐらしの音ぞきこゆなるこやあけぐれと人はいふらむ

honobono ni	Faintly
higurashi no ne zo	The cicada's chirp
kikoyunaru	Comes to my ears;
ko ya akegure to	Now 'tis the dusk before dawn,
hito wa iuramu	So folk do say.

180

With the same conception.

葉を繁み外山の影やまがふらむ明くるも知らぬひぐらしのこゑ

wa o shigemi	So lush with leaves,
toyama no kage ya	Do the nearby mountains' shapes
magauramu	All blend to one, I wonder;
akuru mo shiranu	All unknowing of the light come
higurashi no koe	Cicada chirps.

---

[1] Both Sonohara 園原 and Fuseya 伏屋 were famous poetic locations in Shinano 信濃 province. Sanekata is punning with them as they are homophonous with *sono hara* その腹, 'your belly', and *fuse ya*, 伏せや, 'Let's sleep together'.

181

When Motosuke's daughter[1] was in service to the Empress, we were not especially close, but then became most intimate with each other – a fact which remained unknown to the world at large; our relationship was enduring, but then for one reason or another I did not visit her for a lengthy period; then, when we were engaged in casual conversation, she leaned forward and said, 'You've forgotten me, haven't you!'
I left without reply, but promptly sent her:

忘れずよまたわすれずよかはらやの下たく煙したむせびつゝ

wasurezu yo	I have not forgotten thee,
mata wasurezu yo	Nor will I ever;
kawaraya no	A solid brick-kiln has
shita taku keburi	Kindled beneath it, smoke
shitamusebitsutsu	Smouldering.

182

In reply, from Sei shōnagon:

葦の屋の下たく煙つれなくて絶えざりけるも何によりてぞ

ashi no ya no	A reed-roofed hut with,
shita taku keburi	Kindled beneath it, smoke
tsurenakute	Seems unchanged;
taezarikeru mo	That the flames continue on,
nani ni yorite zo	Pray tell, how should one know it?

---

[1] The daughter of Kiyowara no Motosuke 清原元輔 was the famous diarist Sei shōnagon 清少納言.

183

When Lady Saishō from the Hall of Bright Proclamations had returned to her estate, I called but got the impression that she already had company; returning home, I sent this to her using a woman I had come across washing water-celery[1] in the Nakagawa River.[2]

なかゞはにすゝく田芹のねたき事あらはれてこそあるべかりけれ

nakagawa ni	In Nakagawa
susuku taseri no	Rinsing water-celery
netaki koto	Roots – green-eyed;
arawarete koso	That another had appeared,
arubekarikere	You should have said plainly.

184

To Lady Kojijū,[3] at the palace of the Former Empress.[4]

絶えねとやいかにせよとぞさゝがにのいとかくまでは思はざりしを

taene to ya	We're through – is that it, or
ika ni seyo to zo	What are we to do?
sasagani no	As a spider's
ito kaku made wa	Tangled web
omowazarishi o	I did not think to be.

---

[1] Despite its English name, water-celery, or *seri* 芹 in Japanese, is a member of the parsnip family and produces similar-looking long, white roots, and it is these which the woman is rinsing in the river. The poem puns on *ne taki* 根長き, 'long roots', and *netaki* 嫉き, 'jealousy', hence my usage of 'green-eyed'.

[2] Nakagawa 中川 ('River Naka') was a water course in the north-western part of the capital. Despite its name, the 'river' was only rarely in full flow, and so it poetry it came to be used to symbolise the end of a relationship (*naka* 仲), which is what Sanekata is suggesting to Saishō by his choice of messenger and the reference to the location in his poem.

[3] See poem 81.

[4] This refers to Fujiwara no Noriko (Senshi) 藤原詮子 (962-1001), who had been a consort of Emperor En'yū 円融 (959-991; r. 969-984). After his death, she took orders and was henceforth referred to with the title she is in the original text, *nyōin* 女院, so it seems likely that this poem can be dated to after 991.

185

When I had gone to the palace of the Former Empress to report that I was to leave for the provinces,[1] Jijū the Handmaid[2] said, while providing me with supplies for the journey:

みちのくにころものせきはたちぬれど

>   *michinoku ni*   In Michinoku
>   *koromo no seki wa*   The barrier of garments[3]
>   *tachinuredo*   Will you thread, yet

And I nimbly concluded:

またあふさかはたのもしきかな

>   *mata ausaka wa*   Still, on Meeting Hill[4] is
>   *tanomoshiki kana*   Where I would be.

---

[1] Sanekata was appointed to a post in the government of Michinoku Province and departed on the 27th day of the Ninth Month Chōtoku 長徳 1 [23.10.995], so this exchange probably took place a few days before. Michinoku was famous for its cloth, and the provisions the lady is providing are most likely clothes for the journey, hence the reference to its customs barrier being of garments. 'Meeting Hill' was the barrier affording entrance to the capital, so Sanekata's conclusion says he would far rather remain with the lady in Kyoto, than travel off to the desolate north.

[2] The identity of this woman remains unknown.

[3] Jijū refers to a specific poetic location in her poem, the Barrier of Koromo (*koromo no seki* 衣の関) which is thought to have been located near Hira'izumi in modern Iwate, about sixty kilometres to the north of Sendai. The place name is homophonous with *koromo* 衣 ('clothing'), and hence it was often used to evoke the sense of garments in poetry.

[4] 'Meeting Hill' (*ausaka* 逢坂) lay on the border between Yamashiro 山城 and Ōmi 近江 provinces to the east of the capital. To the court nobility, it marked the border between civilisation and wilderness, and so was frequently used in travel poems. With her opening, Jijū expresses concern for Sanekata in the wilds of Michinoku, while he agrees with his conclusion, that he would rather be returning to the familiar lands of home.

186

On visiting a certain place and hearing some young women chatting from behind the curtains:

すのうちにつゝめく雛のこゑすなり

   su no uchi ni   From within the nest
  tsutsumeku hina no   Chirping chicks'
   koe su nari   Cheeps

I recited this, yet no one replied, so:

かへすほどこそひさしかりけれ

  kaesu hodo koso   Yet hatching
  hisashikarikere   Takes a time, indeed!

187

Though I was victorious when playing Middle Captain Nobukata at *go*, he failed to send over the loser's forfeit, so I wrote this to request it:

かずかずに碁のまけ物をゑてしかなこふにはあらず手うちならはむ

kazukazu ni	Many, indeed, are
go no makemono o	The prizes of *go*
eteshi kana	I would receive;
kou ni wa arazu	I'm not pleading, you understand,
te uchi narawamu	But I had thought to learn a better hand!

The bet was paper, was it not?

188

To a certain lady, on our first morning:

君が宿播磨潟にもあらなくにあかしもはてゞかへりぬるかな

kimi ga yado	Your home, my love,
harimagata ni mo	Upon Harima Beach[1]
aranaku ni	Lies not, yet
akashi mo hatede	Lacking the light of dawn
kaerinuru kana	Have I to my own returned.

189

A fan owned by His Highness, the Crown Prince,[2] had upon it a picture of a cuckoo in flight across Mount Kurahashi,[3] and when many people sent poems to accompany it:

さつきやみ倉橋山のほとゝぎすおぼつかなくもなきわたるかな

satsuki yami	In the Fifth Month's gloom,
kurahashiyama no	On Kurahashi Mountain
hototogisu	A cuckoo
obotsukanaku mo	Faintly
nakiwataru kana	Cries out.

---

[1] Harima 播磨 was a province on the Inland Sea coast to the west of the modern city of Kobe 神戸. It was the location of Akashi 明石, which is homophonous with *akashi* 明し ('be bright') – hence why Sanekata uses it to commence his poem here.

[2] Prince Okisada/Iyasada 居貞, the future Emperor Sanjō 三条 (976-1017; r. 1011-1016).

[3] Mount Kurahashi (*kurahashiyama* 倉橋山) is a poetic location in Yamato 大和 province, a few kilometres to the south east of Sakurai 桜井 in modern Nara prefecture. *Kura* in the place name was homophonous with *kura* 暗 ('dark'), and so it was frequently used to evoke this sense, as in: 倉橋の山を高みか夜隠りに出で来る月の光乏しき *kurahashi no / yama o takami ka / yogomori ni / idekuru tsuki no / hikari tomoshiki* 'Is it Kurahashi / Mountain's height? / In the depths of night / The emerging moon's / Light is feeble, indeed.' (MYS III: 290).

190

From His Excellency,[1] when I became Governor of Michinoku.

この春はいかで睦れん年をへてあひみで戀ひんほどのかたみに

kono haru wa	This spring
ikade mutsuren	Let us be close, for
toshi o hete	Years will pass
aimide koin	Without a glimpse; of fond
hodo no katami ni	Times let this be a keepsake.

191

My reply:

なにゝかは君にむつれて年をへば衣の關を思ひたゝまし

nani ni ka wa	How,
kimi ni mutsurete	Being in my lord's fond regard
toshi o eba	These years past,
koromo no seki o	The barrier of garments
omoi tatamashi	Can I think to thread?

---

[1] Probably a reference to Fujiwara no Michitaka 藤原道隆 (953-995). Contemporary sources describe Michitaka as a generous and talkative man, who was fond of drinking to excess and often did so with Naritoki, Sanekata's uncle, and Fujiwara no Asamitsu 藤原朝光, both of whom died earlier in 995. He is reputed to have said that the only reason he recited the *nembutsu* 念仏, the name of Amida Buddha, in his final days was so that he could be reunited with his drinking companions in paradise after his death.

192

When I was leaving for Michinoku, Lord Yorimitsu[1] came to visit; he dropped his fan and I returned it with this.

目のまへにまづも忘るゝ扇かなわかれはこゝろうしろめたけれ

me no mae ni	Right before my eyes
mazu mo wasururu	First forgotten is
augi kana	This fan;
wakare wa kokoro	Parting is, indeed, a heart's
ushirometakere	Grief.

193

His reply.

身のならむかたも知られぬ別れにはまして扇のゆくへまでには

mi no naramu	What I should do
kata mo shirarenu	I know not at all upon
wakare ni wa	Our parting;
mashite augi no	Truly, for my fan's
yukue made ni wa	Location I care not!

194

To Emon, at Koichijō.[2]

目の前に絶えせず見ゆるつらさかな憂きを昔と思ふべき世に

me no mae ni	Before my eyes
taesezu miyuru	Endless seems
tsurasa kana	Your spite;
uki o mukashi to	Cruelty in the past
omoubeki yo ni	Should be, in this world of ours.

---

[1] Minamoto no Yorimitsu 源頼光 (d.1021).
[2] The Koichijō 小一条 mansion was the home of Sanekata's uncle, Naritoki. Emon was a lady-in-waiting there.

195

On returning a fan[1] to the same lady, around autumn.

秋はてぬいまは扇もかへしてむなを頼むかと人もこそみれ

aki hatenu
ima wa augi mo
kaeshitemu
nao tanomu ka to
hito mo koso mire

Autumn's longings are at an end, so
Now, your fan
I do return, lest
Further entreaties to make
I have – or so you'd think!

196

Her reply.

秋はてゝ扇かへすは憂けれどもさすがに忌むと見るぞうれしき

aki hatete
augi kaesu wa
ukeredomo
sasugani imu to
miru zo ureshiki

That autumn and your longings are done, and
To have my fan returned
Is bitter, indeed, yet,
As expected, to be shunned by you:
Now that is a pleasant thought, indeed!

---

[1] If a man took a lady's fan, it was considered a promise that he would come back and visit her again. Sending it back, as Sanekata is doing here, was a sign that he had lost interest in her and the relationship was over. As you can tell from this, the previous poem and Emon's reply, their relationship did not end amicably.

197

When I had gone to the house of the same Shōjō,[1] and she had sent me home without meeting me.

命だにあらばたのまむ逢ふことのいといきがたきこゝちこそすれ

inochi dani	Long life
araba tanomamu	Had I, yearn
au koto no	To meet with you I would, but
ito ikigataki	How hard it is to go on
kokochi koso sure	Feeling as I do.

198

To a certain lady, at an Uji estate.[2]

橋姫の片敷く袖も片敷かでおもはざりつるものをこそおもへ

hashihime no	The Goddess of the Bridge,[3]
katashiku sode mo	Spreads single sleeves and sleeps
katashikade	alone;
omowazaritsuru	Without you
mono o koso omoe	I had not thought
	To feel this way.

---

[1] See Poem 84.

[2] Various members of the higher nobility had estates at Uji 宇治, a short distance from the capital, but the exact location referred to here remains unknown.

[3] The bridge across the Uji river was particularly famous, and its guardian deity, Uji no Hashihime 宇治の橋姫, was addressed or referred to in many poems.

199

On the Sixth Day of the Seventh Month,[1] I met a lady for the first time; the following morning:

七夕は今日をや昨日まちわびしわれは昨日ぞ今日は戀ふらし

      tanabata wa   The Weaver Maid,
      kyō o ya kinō   Yesterday, for today
      machiwabishi   Spent longing;
      ware wa kinō zo   I, of yesterday,
      kyō wa kourashi   Today think fondly.

200

Her reply:

彦星の心も知らぬ七夕は昨日も今日もゝのぞくやしき

      hikoboshi no   The Herd Boy's
      kokoro mo shiranu   Heart unknown is to
      tanabata wa   The Weaver Maid;
      kinō mo kyō mo   Yesterday and today both,
      mono zo kuyashiki   All is most vexatious!

---

[1] The day before the celebration of the Tanabata 七夕 festival commemorating the annual meeting of the celestial lovers, the Weaver Maid and the Herd Boy (the stars Altair and Vega).

201

Lord Sanemasa[1] wrote begging some daywear when he was to go to Harima, and I sent it, saying:

あまたゝびたちなれにけるかりごろもたむけの神も心はづかし

amata tabi	Time and again on journeys
tachinarenikeru	Do you depart, so familiar
karigoromo	Are these clothes
tamuke no kami mo	That before your guardian God[2]
kokoro hazukashi	I feel my shame.

202

I entered the chambers of a certain lady whom the Major Captain[3] had previously visited and, not leaving, after about two days:

うきにかく戀しきこともありけるをいさつらからむいかゞ思ふと

uki ni kaku	For you to be so cold,
koishiki koto mo	When such love
arikeru o	I have for you;
isa tsurakaramu	Should I be hard-hearted, too –
ikaga omou to	What think you, my lady?

203

To a certain lady, while the Major Captain was ill.

みづからは思ひわづらふともなきにあはぬばかりやくるしかるらむ

mizukara wa	I,
omoiwazurau	Sick at heart
tomonaki ni	Am not, yet
awanu bakari ya	Simply not meeting you:
kurushikaruramu	Can it truly cause such pain?

---

[1] Fujiwara no Sanemasa 藤原信理 is known to have gone to Harima in 991, dating this poem to that year.

[2] It was good manners in ancient Japan, as it still is today, to play down the significance and quality of any gift made to another.

[3] Sanekata's uncle, Fujiwara no Naritoki.

204

And again to the lady:

そへてまたあはぬめをさへ嘆くかなもの思ふときはまことなりけり

soete mata / *awanu me o sae* / *nageku kana* / *mono'omou toki wa* / *makoto narikeri*

soete mata	What's more,
awanu me o sae	I cannot close my eyes at all,
nageku kana	Such is my grief;
mono'omou toki wa	That my gloomy thoughts are so
makoto narikeri	Is true, I tell you.

205

When the Major Captain passed away,[1] at around the same time:

人しれずぬれし袂は墨染にそめてもそへてものをこそ思へ

hito sirezu	Secretly, unknown to all,
nureshi tamoto wa	Soaked were your sleeves,
sumizome ni	Upon Ink-dark
sometemo soete	Mourning shades:
mono o koso omoe	Black, indeed, I feel!

---

[1] Naritoki died on the 23rd day of the Fourth Month, Chōtoku 長徳 1 [25.5.995].

206

At around the time when my visits to Lady Emon at Koichijō[1] became sporadic, I went to visit her by ox-cart, with my ox-boy, Akimaro, as an outcrier; at her estate, the lady:

雲居にて鳴きわたりなるかりがねは秋こし路や思ひいづらん

kumoi nite	Above the clouds,[2]
nakiwatarinaru	Known to squawk is
kari ga ne wa	The gander:
aki kosi michi ya	Now autumn longings have come, the wa
omoi izuran	Here has he recalled?

207

My reply:

歸る雁いづちかゆかむ住みなれしきみが常世の國ならずして

kaeru kari	Homeward bound, the gander:
izuchi ka yukamu	Where should he go, indeed?
suminareshi	If not the familiar,
kimi ga tokoyo no	Eternal, unchanging
kuni narazushite	Land[3] of his lady!

---

[1] See poem 194.
[2] Emon's poems contains a number of double meanings: 'above the clouds' *kumoi* 雲居, was a standard euphemism for the palace and court, while the reference to the goose's call referred to Sanekata's reputation for being unfaithful. *Aki* is simultaneously 'autumn', 'longing' and evokes the name of Sanekata's ox-boy, Akimaro. Essentially, then, the lady is saying, "You've got a name at court for being unfaithful (and now you have the gall) to come visit, just because you feel like it (after so long: how dare you!)"
[3] Sanekata's reply contains some wordplay of his own, in that *toko* was simultaneously 'eternal' and 'bed'. So, his reply means, "There is nowhere I could possibly be, except your bed, of which I have become so fond!"

208

Sent on the first day of the Fourth Month[1] to Middle Captain Nobukata, while in mourning for my aunt.

薄しとや人のみるとて墨染のころもは夏もしられざりけり

<table>
<tr><td>usushi to ya</td><td>How unlucky, it is</td></tr>
<tr><td>hito no miru tote</td><td>For folk to see me so;</td></tr>
<tr><td>sumizome no</td><td>Ink-stained</td></tr>
<tr><td>koromo wa natsu mo</td><td>Clothes, of summer are</td></tr>
<tr><td>shirarezarikeri</td><td>Quite unaware.</td></tr>
</table>

209

Sent to the grandfather, a man whose daughter had died, on seeing how fond he was of his grandchild.

いにしへの形見にこれや山賤の撫でゝおはせる常夏の花

<table>
<tr><td>inishie no</td><td>Of times gone-by</td></tr>
<tr><td>katami ni kore ya</td><td>Here is but a keepsake:</td></tr>
<tr><td>yamagatsu no</td><td>A woodsman's</td></tr>
<tr><td>nadete ōseru</td><td>Carefully tended</td></tr>
<tr><td>tokonatsu no hana</td><td>Pink.</td></tr>
</table>

---

[1] The first day of the Fourth Month was the official date for nobles to change into summer clothing; Sanekata, however, being in mourning, would not be changing out of his 'ink-stained' black robes.

210

When I was to go to Michinoku, Kintō, the Director of the Bureau of the Palace Guards,[1] sent me this to say he would present me with a saddle cloth.

東路の木の下暗くなりゆかば都の月を戀ひざらめやは

azumaji no	If on the eastern roads
ko no shita kuraku	Beneath the trees should darkness
nariyukaba	Fall,
miyako no tsuki o	Of the moonlit capital
koizarame ya wa	Might you not think fondly?

211

My reply:

ことつてむ都のかたへ行く人に木の下暗にいとゞ惑ふと

kototetemu	Tell this,
miyako no kata e	To all capital
yuku hito ni	Bound folk:
ko no shitakura ni	In the dark beneath the trees,
itodo modou to	I wander, completely lost.

212

From Middle Captain Taka'ie:[2]

別れ路はいつもなげきのつきせぬにいとゞわびしき秋の夕ぐれ

wakareji wa	On a path of parting
itsumo nageki no	Grief ever has
tsukisenu ni	No end, yet
itodo wabishiki	How my loneliness grows
aki no yūgure	This autumn eve.

---

[1] See poem 135.
[2] Fujiwara no Taka'ie 藤原隆家 (979-1044). Taka'ie was made Middle Captain of the Inner Palace Guards, Right Division (*ukonoe chūjō* 右近衛中将) on the 9th day of the Third Month, Shōryaku 正暦 4 [3.4.993] and promoted to Supernumerary Middle Counsellor (*gonchūnagon* 権中納言) on the 6th day of the Fourth Month, Chōtoku 長徳 1 [8.5.995], dating Taka'ie's poem to this two year period.

213

My reply (probably sent around the end of the Ninth Month):

白雲のたなびくかたはこゆれどもわかれの空に惑ふころかな

    shirakumo no   Where white clouds
    tanabiku kata wa   Stream, I have
    koyuredomo   Passed by, yet
    wakare no sora ni   Having parted, beneath such skies
    madou koro kana   Am I lost, indeed.

214

From the lady in the Hall of Bright Proclamations,[1] with some traveling clothes.

見ぬほどのかたみに添ふる心あるをあくなとぞおもふ筥潟の磯

    minu hodo no   While we cannot meet
    katami ni souru   Let these be a keepsake close
    kokoro aru o   By your heart;
    aku na to zo omou   Open not to other thoughts of me,
    hakokata no iso   Boxed by the stony shore of
                                                             Hakokata.[2]

---

[1] The identity of this woman remains unknown.
[2] *Hakokata no iso* 筥潟の磯 ('the stony shore of Hakokata'): this *utamakura* is thought to have been located in Michinoku, possibly near the barrier at Shirakawa (see poem 177) and, despite its name to refer not to a seashore, but the banks of a river, pond, or marsh, but its actual location has not been identified.

215

My reply, sent to the lady before departure, out of thanks for her consideration.

心にもあらぬ別れを筥潟のいそぐをかつはうらみつるかな

kokoro ni mo   Deep within my heart
aranu wakare o   This parting does not lie, yet
hakokata no   To Hakokata's
isogu o katsu wa   Stony shore to be hastened is
uramitsuru kana   another
     Cause for sorrow!

216

From the Crown Prince,[1] sent to the place I was staying before departure[2] and written by the Ukon Chamberlain.[3]

わかれぢの涙に袖もさそはれていかなる道にとまらざるらむ

wakareji no   On the way of parting
namida ni sode mo   Tears on to sleeves
sasowarete   Are drawn,
ikanaru michi ni   Is there any path
tomarazuramu   To stop them, I wonder?

---

[1] Prince Okisada/Iyasada 居貞, the future Emperor Sanjō 三条 (976-1017; r. 1011-1016).

[2] Travelling in Heian Japan was fraught with danger and in order to avoid misfortune it was vital to only depart on appropriately propitious days and from directions which would avoid offending supernatural forces. This meant that travellers often left their homes and stayed elsewhere for a few days, so that their 'official' departures would provide the best luck.

[3] The commentators suggest that Sanekata has misidentified the writer of this letter. Sanjō's lady chamberlain was, in fact, Sakon 左近, and not Ukon 右近, so it would seem he has simply miswritten the lady's name Inukai Kiyoshi, Gotō Shōko and Hirano Yukiko (1994) Heian Shika Shū. *Shin Nihon Koten Bungaku Taikei*. Tokyo: Iwanami Shoten..

217

Departing the capital and staying on the riverside at a place called Mitoshigawa,¹ the moon was resting on the surface of the river.

月かげも旅の空とやおもふらん三としのかはのそこにやどれる

tsukikage mo	The moonlight, too,
tabi no sora to ya	Does it journey from the skies,
omouran	I wonder;
mitoshi no kawa no	Upon Mitoshi's River
soko ni yadoreru	Bed to find lodging…

218

Sent from Michinoku to Middle Captain Nobukata.

やすらはず思ひたちにし東路にありけるものをはばかりの關

yasurawazu	Unhesitating
omoi tachinishi	Did I depart
azumaji ni	Upon the Eastern roads
arikeru mono o	To hesitate before the
habakari no seki	Barrier of Habakari!²

---

[1] This location has not been satisfactorily identified.
[2] The Barrier of Habakari (*habakari no seki* 憚関), was located in Michinoku in the north of Japan. Its primary use in poetry, though was as a play on words, in that *habakari*, also meant 'hesitation'.

219

Masahira, Senior Assistant Minister of Ceremonial,[1] sent this to me in Michinoku.

都にはたれをか君は思ふらん都にはみな君を戀ふめり

miyako ni wa	Within the Capital
tare o ka kimi wa	Who is it you
omouran	Hold dear?
miyako ni wa mina	Within the Capital everyone
kimi o koumeri	For you is longing, it seems.

220

My reply.

忘られぬ人のうちには忘れぬを戀ふらむ人のうちに待つやは

wasurarenu	Among unforgettable
hito no uchi ni wa	Folk, you
wasurenu o	Can I forget the least;
kouramu hito no	Among those longing,
uchi ni matsu ya wa	I wonder, do you await me most?

---

[1] Ōe no Masahira 大江匡衡 (952-1012). Masahira was a poet and Confucian scholar and was numbered among the Later Thirty Six Poetic Immortals by Fujiwara no Norikane 藤原範兼 (1107-1165). He had seven poems included in the *Goshūishū* 後拾遺集 imperial poetry anthology, and a further twelve in later ones. Today, he is chiefly remembered as the husband of a much greater poet, Akazome emon 赤染衛門 (956?-1041?) – by all accounts they were a most affectionate and happily married couple – and as the victim of an assault in 985, which severed the fingers of his right hand. His assailant is believed to have been Fujiwara no Yasusuke 藤原 保輔 (-988), a notorious criminal who was eventually tracked down to a temple where he had attempted to evade arrest by taking orders after committing a burglary. He attempted suicide when his capture was inevitable, and died in prison the following day.

221

In Michinoku, after my wife had died, I wrote this when Tsutsugimi[1] put on trousers for the first time.[2]

いにしへをけふにあはするものならばひとりは千代を祈らざらまし

inishie o
kyō ni awasuru
mono naraba
hitori wa chiyo o
inorazaramashi

If she, now gone,
To meet with this day
Had been able,
Alone, for a thousand years of health
I would not be praying…

222

At the Shirakawa Estate, early one morning at the beginning of Spring.

吹風になみの心やかよふらむ春立つ今日の白川の水

fuku kaze ni
nami no kokoro ya
kayouramu
haru tatsu kyō no
shirakawa no mizu

Is it that in the gusting wind
Waves' spirits
Travel?
On this first day of Spring
White are the waters of Shirakawa.

---

[1] Sanekata's son: see poem 164.
[2] This is a reference to *hakamagi* 袴着, a ceremony which took place, usually at about the age of three, when an child made the change from infant's to child's clothing.

223

On hearing a cuckoo in deep in a forest of cedars.

羽振きつゝ今や都へほとゝぎす過ぎ難に鳴く杉叢の森

habukitsutsu	Wings beating,
ima ya miyako e	Capital-bound is
hototogisu	The cuckoo, yet
suginade ni naku	Loath to leave, he cries
sugimura no mori	Deep among the cedar trees.

224

After viewing blossoms with a certain lady, the following day, she sent:

とまるやと惜しみし花を君かとて名殘をのみぞ今日はながむる

tomaru ya to	'Could you stay awhile?'
oshimishi hana o	Wistful, of the blossoms, did I
kimi ka tote	wonder;
nagori o nomi zo	'And what of you, my lord?'
kyō wa nagamuru	Vestiges are all
	I gaze upon today.

225

In reply:

むべしこそかへりし空もかすみつゝ花のあたりは立ち憂かりしか

mube shi koso	Indeed!
kaerishi sora mo	Homeward bound, the heavens
kasumitsutsu	Hazed were;
hana no atari wa	From beside such a blossom,
tachi ukarishika	'Tis painful to part.

226

風をいたみ本荒の萩の露だにもあはれいかなる人を待つらむ

kaze o itami	Biting is the wind upon
motoara no hagi no	The sparse bush clover;[1]
tsuyu dani mo	Even a dewdrop there
aware ikanaru	Sadly, for someone
hito o matsuramu	Seems to wait…

227

After speaking with a women, the following day I sent this attached to a pink,[2] and what do you think happened?

とこなつの花の露にはむつれねどぬるともなくて濡れし袖かな

tokonatsu no	Well-bedded, the pink
hana no tsuyu ni wa	Flower's dewfall:
mutsurenedo	Intimate with it I'm not, yet
	Unsuspecting,
nurutomonakute	How drenched have my
nureshi sode kana	sleeves become!

---

[1] Bush clover (*hagi* 萩; *Lespedeza bicolour*) is a flowering shrub closely associated with autumn in Japanese poetry. This seasonal association also included linking the plant with the dew that settled upon it, which is a familiar trope Sanekata uses here.

[2] Pinks (*tokonatsu* 常夏; *Dianthus*) were frequently used as a metaphor for a young woman, as Sanekata does in his poem here. It was normal courtly practice to attach love letters to flowers, or sprigs of blossom, in order to reinforce and heighten their aesthetic effect.

228

In reply to what was written by the Gentleman-in-Waiting to the Lay Priest[1] upon a silver water-horn,[2] when I was to go down to Usa.[3]

むすぶ手の別れとおもふにいとゞしくこのみづゝのに袖ぞ濡れける

musubu te no Our clasped hands
wakare to omou ni Parting, were in my thoughts, so
itodoshiku Certain it was that
kono mizutsuno ni This water-horn would
sode zo nurekeru Soak my sleeves.

229

When the moon was shining brightly and I was conversing with a lady, we heard the plovers call:

濱千鳥いづこに鳴くぞ月まつと

hama chidori Plovers on the beach:
izuko ni naku zo Where do they cry?
tsuki matsu to While waiting for the moon…

I said, and she concluded:

あかしの浦とおもふなるべし

akashi no ura to Bright Akashi Bay[4]
omounarubeshi Must be their thought!

---

[1] There is some doubt as to the identity of this person, but the most likely candidate is Fujiwara no Suketō 藤原相任, one of Sanekata's cousins, who finally took orders in 986.

[2] A 'water-horn' (*mizutsuno* 水角) was a traditional parting gift given to travellers. It is believed to have often contained gold-dust Inukai Kiyoshi, Gotō Shōko and Hirano Yukiko (1994) Heian Shika Shū. *Shin Nihon Koten Bungaku Taikei*. Tokyo: Iwanami Shoten., and so would have been a way of providing additional funds for a journey. With his poem, Sanekata metaphorically draws upon the image of an over-spilling drinking vessel to allude to the tears of grief he is shedding at the thought of parting from his friend.

[3] This refers to Sanekata's visit to Usa Shrine in 983 as an imperial messenger. See poem 1 for details.

[4] The place name Akashi 明石 was homophonous with the adjective *akashi* 明し ('be bright'), and so was frequently used with this dual meaning.

230

When I had a passion for a lady at the palace, and she had said she might meet me herself, but had left without sending word.

おもへ君ちぎらぬ宵の月だにも人に知られで出づるものかは

omoe kimi	Think on this, my lady!
chigiranu yoi no	Footloose in the night is
tsuki dani mo	The moon; would even she,
hito ni shirarede	Telling not a soul,
izuru mono ka wa	Depart?

231

To the same lady, to say how much I had relied upon her.

今日今日と人をたのめぬ山の端もかくや月日をすぐしきぬらむ

kyō kyō to	'Today is the day!' I hoped;
hito o tanomenu	None such for
yama no wa mo	The mountains' edge which
kaku ya tsuki hi o	Just so sees the moon and sun
sugushikinuramu	Pass by…

232

When I had sent a letter to the same lady and not received a reply.

こはさらにいる山水のをしどりのをしとやあとを見せずなりぬる

ko wa sara ni	Once again, must
iru yamamizu no	The tarn-dwelling
oshidori no	Mandarin duck[1]
oshi to ya ato o	Regret, that of tracks[2]
misezu narinuru	He catches not a glimpse?

---

[1] Mandarin ducks, or *oshidori* 鴛鴦 in Japanese, were used as a standard metaphor for faithfulness because they mated for life. Here, Sanekata is not only using the word in this sense, but also to introduce the following adjective *oshi* 惜し 'regret'.

[2] 'Tracks' (*ato* 跡) were a standard metaphor for writing. The mandarin duck, unable to see the tracks of his mate on the surface of their mountain tarn, is Sanekata, searching in vain for a letter from his lover.

233

The same lady married the Major Captain and so I was unable to meet her again; after considerable effort I spoke with her and, the following morning:

いそのかみふるき道とは知りながらまどふばかりぞ今日は戀しき

iso no kami	The stone-clad
furuki michi to wa	Ancient path:
shirinagara	I know it well, yet
madou bakari zo	Lost am I upon it
kyō wa koishiki	This morning in my yearning.

234

When I had sent a letter to the Taira Handmaid,[1] and received no reply.

かきくらしふる沫雪の袖ふかみけふくものあとの見えじとすらむ

kakikurashi	Blinding,
furu awayuki no	Falls a gentle snow,
sode fukami	Drifting upon my sleeves;
kyō kumo no ato no	Today, the clouds not a single
mieji to suramu	trace
	Have shown.

---

[1] Possibly Taira no Takako 平貴子 (dates unknown), who was appointed Secretary of the Handmaid's Office (*naishi no jō* 掌侍) on the 8th day of the Fifth Month Tengen 天元 5 [2.6.982], and was a lady-in-waiting to Fujiwara no Nobuko (Junshi) 藤原遵子 (957-1017), the consort of Emperor En'yū 円融.

235

Sent to a woman to say how much I wanted to meet her, when I had gone to Hatsuse:[1]

石上布留の瀬川の水たえて妹にあはずてとほどぞへにける

iso no kami	Stone-bound and
furu no segawa no	Ancient, the rapids'
mizu taete	Waters ever are;
imo ni awazute	Without you, darling,
hodo zo henikeru	An age has passed.

236

Written on the back of a letter from a certain lady who had written to me most fondly, when I discovered it long after our relationship was over:

いかなりしときの水茎かゝりけむとみればたえてものぞかなしき

ika narishi	How was it in
toki no mizuguki	Those times for such an outflow
kakarikemu	To be here?
to mireba taete	Now the sight, truly,
mono zo kanashiki	Leaves me all forlorn.

237

When I said to this lady, 'Night is almost over, and I should leave you.'

秋風の小夜更けがたにをとのせば必ず問へよわれと答えん

aki kaze no	Autumn winds,
sayo fukegata ni	At a brief night's dawning,
oto noseba	Gust on;
kanarazu toe yo	Pay heed! For
ware to kotaen	They say, 'It's me.'

---

[1] Hatsuse was the location of Hasedera 長谷寺, a major Buddhist temple. Sanekata would have gone there on a pilgrimage.

238

When the Taira Handmaid had not replied to me, I took a letter that she had sent to someone's house on some matter of business and, cutting out some words,[1] sent them to her.

伊勢をのや海人と我身はなりぬらん袖のうらなる涙かこへば

ise ono ya	An Ise fisher
ama to wagami wa	Man have I
narinuran	Become?
sode no uranaru	My undersleeves
namida kakoeba	Bounded by tears…

239

When I had gone to a lady's house and another man had arrived after me, the lady sent him home and while she played a zither:[2]

人知れずかへれることを聞くからに人の上ともおもほへぬかな

hito shirezu	A stranger,
kaereru koto o	Change of tone, go home
kiku kara ni	I hear;
hito no ue to mo	Another man –
omōenu kana	I had no idea…

---

[1] The words Sanekata cuts out are not explicitly mentioned, but the commentators suggest that he may have cut out the expression *mitsu to dani* 見つとだに ('if only I had seen you'), as similar behaviour is attested in other sources Inukai Kiyoshi, Gotō Shōko and Hirano Yukiko (1994) *Heian Shika Shū. Shin Nihon Koten Bungaku Taikei*. Tokyo: Iwanami Shoten..

[2] Sanekata's original contains some rather clever wordplay in that *kaereru koto* is both 'the fact of having sent (someone) home' and 'changing a zither's tone'. The change, of course, is also in the lady, who has been entertaining another lover.

240

Sent to a lady on the first day of the Fourth Month.[1]

夏衣うすき頼みに頼ませて厚き衣を更へやしてまし

natsu koromo	Summer garb
usuki tanomi ni	Is light[2] I'm surely
tanomasete	Certain;
atsuki koromo o	These heavy robes,
kae ya shitemashi	I wonder: should I change them?

241

When I knocked upon the door of the chamber of a lady at the palace, with whom I had spoken before, she said:

誰そやこの鳴戸の下に音するは

taso ya kono	Who is it,
naruto no shita ni	At these straits
oto suru wa	A'sounding?

I replied:

とまりもとむる海人の釣り舟

tomari mo tomuru	A port a'seeking
ama no tsurinbune	Fisher boat!

---

[1] The first day of the Fourth Month (approximately mid-May) was the official date for changing out of winter clothes and into summer ones.

[2] Sanekata is referring to: Topic unknown.夏衣薄きながらぞ頼まるゝ一重なるしも身に近ければ *natsu koromo / usukinagara zo / tanomaruru / hitoe narusi mo / mi ni chikakereba* 'Summer garb / Is light, indeed, yet / How sure I was with / A single layer / Close against me.' Anonymous (SIS XIII: 832) here. 'Light summer garb' *usuki natsu koromo* was commonly used in love poetry, both to imply the lightness of a lover's regard and skin-to-skin contact between lovers. In his poem, Sanekata says, 'I know you may not care for me, but what about getting together?'

242

Then, the lady:

狭衣にかたしく袖のつゆけきをいかにしてかは君に貸すべき

sagoromo ni	My night-robe's
katashiku sode no	Single sleeve is
tsuyukeki o	Wet with dew;
ika ni shite ka wa	Why
kimi ni kasubeki	Would I lend it you, my lord?

243

Sent to a lady on the day of the first snowfall of the year.

あひ思はぬ人の心に淡雪のとけてしのぶる我やなになり

aiomowanu	A callous
hito no kokoro ni	Heart's passions as
awayuki no	Sleeting snow
tokete shinoburu	Do melt away; and for long-suffering
ware ya nani nari	Me, what's left?

244

To the same woman, on hearing that she had been speaking to another.

むすぶ手のしづくに濁るきみよりもあかずも聞きし君が聲かな

musubu te no	Entwined hands
shizuku ni nigoru	Beaded, sullied
kimi yori mo	You, yet
akazu mo kikishi	All I wished was
kimi ga koe kana	To hear your voice once more.

245

When someone had sent me some paper as a response.

年を經ていのるしるしはちはやぶるかみもあはれときかざらめやは

    toshi o hete   Over many passing years
 inoru shirushi wa   Have I prayed for a sign:
    chihayaburu   The mighty
 kami mo aware to   Gods, fondly,
 kikazarame ya wa   Have heard me not, it seems…

246

Then, when I had said, 'What sort of a reply is that?'

あはれてふ言の葉いかでみてしかなわびはつる身のなぐさめにせむ

    aware chō   A kind
 koto no wa ikade   Word: how much
    miteshi kana   I wanted it;
 wabiwatsuru mi no   Gaunt from grief,
 nagusame ni semu   A consolation it would be…

247

On the first day of the First Month.

今日よりはひとへにたのむわぎもこが身をむつましみ衣たつとて

    kyō yori wa   Today
 hitoe ni tanomu   In you is all my trust;
    wagimoko ga   My darling,
 mi o mutsumashimi   Think fond thoughts and
 koromo tatsu tote   Sew a single robe for me.

248

When I had been conversing with a lady through a slightly open door, I fastened this to the hem of her robe.

いにしへもちぎる心に結びけむ衣のつまはとくやとけずや

inishie mo	In ancient times
chigiru kokoro ni	A bond between two hearts
musubikemu	Laced
koromo no tsuma wa	A skirt hem
toku ya tokezu ya	Would come undone, or would it not?

249

Sent to a lady when I had heard that another man had written to her while she was in the birthing hut.

うしろめた一言主やいかならむたへまにわぶる久米の岩橋

ushirometa	Uneasy am I:
hitokotonushi ya	The Master of a Single Word
ika naramu	Is up to something…
tae ma ni waburu	Our time apart is a rift as in
kume no iwabashi	Kume's unfinished bridge of stone.[1]

---

[1] See poem 107.

250

When I had begun speaking to the Junior Assistant Handmaid,[1] and our relationship was a great secret.

忍び音も苦しきものをほととぎすいざ卯の花のかげにかくれむ

shinobine mo	A whispered secret night together
kurushiki mono o	Is wretched, indeed, so
hototogisu	Cuckoo,
iza u no hana no	Let us, in the summer snow
kage ni kakuremu	blooms' Shade, find shelter.

251

When a lady was returning to her estates and I had said I wished to speak with her, but we were unable to meet, I sent this to her house the following morning.

風をいたみ船出し野田の海人よりも静心なきめをもみるかな

kaze o itami	Cruel blows the wind on
funadeshi noda no	Ships setting sail; Noda's[2]
ama yori mo	Fisherfolk have less
shizukokoronaki	Unquiet hearts and
me o mo miru kana	Suffer less than I.

---

[1] The identity of this lady has not been definitively determined, but it is possible that she was the daughter of the wet nurse to Fujiwara no Akiko (Senshi) 藤原詮子 (962-991), a consort of emperor En'yū, who is known to have held this position at around this time.

[2] Noda 野田 was a minor poetic location (*utamakura*) in Michinoku in the north of Japan.

252

When a lady was ill, and I had not been to see her for a long time, I wrote this, telling her to look at the edge.[1]

戀しともえやはいぶきのさしも草よそにもゆれどかひなかりけり

koishitomo	I yearn for you yet,
e ya wa ibuki no	I cannot say: on Mount Ibuki[2]
sashimogusa	Scrubby mugwort
yoso no moyuredo	Burns far away, though
kainakarikeri	'Tis no avail…

253

When a lady had a previous lover, and it was difficult to speak with her.

暮れにもと言ふべきものを大堰川井堰の水は漏るや漏らずや

kure ni mo to	Even were it eventide,
iubeki mono o	There are words I'd say to you;
ōigawa	The River Ōi's[3]
iseki no mizu wa	Dam-stopped waters:
moru ya morazu ya	Will they overflow, or will they not?[4]

---

[1] Exactly what Sanekata means here remains obscure. The commentators suggestion is that he is telling her to look at the margin of his letter to her where he may have written the poem.
[2] See poem 121.
[3] The Ōi River (ōigawa 大堰川) was the name given to the upper reaches of the Katsura River (katsuragawa 桂川) before it reached the west of the capital. The nobility frequently visited it on pleasure trips and hence it became a poetic location, frequently associated with torchlit cormorant fishing, although here Sanekata takes advantage of the fact that the wi in the river's name was sometimes written with the character 堰, meaning dam.
[4] In other words, 'I am worried lest word of our affair gets back to your other man.'

254

To the same lady, when, yet again, I could not meet her.

ながむるを頼むものにて明かしてきたゞかたぶきしの月の影見て

nagamuru o	That you, too, gaze
tanomu mono nite	I trust, and now
akashiteki	The night is lightening, with
tada katabukishi no	Only the waning
tsuki no kage mite	Moonlight for company.

255

On the seventh day,[1] when it was still difficult to meet.

逢ふことを人に貸すともおもはぬにそらにきこゆるいづれなるらん

au koto o	That our meeting
hito ni kasu tomo	To another would you give
omowanu ni	I think not, yet
sora ni kikoyuru	From the skies I hear,
izure naruran	'Which one shall it be…?'

256

When I had gone to Kogawa,[2] a lady's father, thinking I was Governor of Ki:

風はやみ吹上の濱のかたさらに思こゝろにくらべても見む

kaze hayami	Fierce is the wind
fukiage no hama no	Across the beach at Fukiage[3]
kata sara ni	Strand, yet
omou kokoro ni	With my thought-filled heart
kurabete mo mimu	Compare it—why don't you!

---

[1] Of the Seventh Month – Tanabata. Sanekata is placing himself in the role of the Herd Boy and his lover in that of the Weaver Maid, but suggesting that the lady is pondering which of her two lovers to meet, unlike the ever-faithful Weaver Maid.

[2] This is a reference to Kogawa temple (*kogawadera* 粉河寺) in Ki 紀 province about a hundred kilometres to the south of the capital – a considerable distance. The temple was dedicated to the bodhisattva of mercy, Kannon, and was a destination for pilgrimages.

[3] Fukiage Beach (*fukiage no hama* 吹上の濱) was a poetic location in Ki province, renowned for the strength of the wind that blew across if from the sea.

257

When a lady had gone to Hase[1] and was returning, I sent someone to say that we could meet where she was and, indeed, we did.

こゝながら袖ぞつゆけき草枕十市の里の旅寝とおもへば

koko nagara
sode zo tsuyukeki
kusamakura
tōchi no sato no
tabine to omoeba

Here,
My sleeves are dew-drenched, indeed:
Pillowed on the grasses,
At Tōchi hamlet[2] and
Slumbering on your travels—how you fill my thoughts…

258

On the fifth day of the month,[3] when I had last met her on the second.

逢はぬまのみぎはに生ふるあやめ草ねのみなかるゝ昨日今日かな

awanu ma no
migiwa ni ouru
ayamegusa
ne nomi nakaruru
kinō kyō kana

Time is a marsh without you;
Sprouting by the water's edge
The sweet flags,
Roots washed—in sobs alone
Did I pass yesterday, and today, too.

---

[1] This was an alternative name for Hatsuse. See poem 235.

[2] Tōchi 十市 was an *utamakura* in Yamashiro 山城 province, referring to an area to the south of modern Nara which was the location of a number of famous mountains, including Mount Kagu 香久, which was often mentioned in early poetry. Tōchi was primarily used by poets to add an image of distance, as, when written in syllabic script as とをち, it was identical to *tōji* 遠路 ('distant roads') - hence Sanekata's reference to travel at the end of his poem.

[3] A reference to the fifth day of the Fifth Month, the day of the Sweet Flag festival, when the plants were hung from the eaves of houses to ward off illness.

259

When I had said, 'I want to speak with you,' and by the time she had said, 'Come now!' dawn had broken, the following morning:

露はらふ人しなければ冬の夜にをきあかしつるほど知らなむ

   tsuyu harau   To brush away the dewfall
 hito shinakereba   I have no one, so
   fuyu no yo ni   This winter's night
  oki akashitsuru   I was awake till dawn;
 hodo o shiranamu   I would have you know how long it was!

260

On a day when I had been visiting temples, to the Captain of the Outer Palace Guards:[1]

いそがなむ散りもこそすれもみぢするまさきのかづら遅くゝるとて

    isoganamu   Make haste!
 chiri mo koso sure   For they will fall,
   momiji suru   Taking on autumn shades,
 masaki no kazura   The evergreen creepers,
  osoku kuru tote   Should you dally more!

---

[1] It is unclear to whom Sanekata is referring here, although both Fujiwara no Kintō and Fujiwara no Michinaga have been suggested by the commentators.

261

When I had been speaking with Lady Hyōe,[1] in service to the Empress, and she had withdrawn extremely early, the following morning:

久かたの天のとながら見し月の飽かで入りにし空ぞこひしき

hisakata no	The eternal
ama no to nagara	Gates of Heaven these are not, yet
mishi tsuki no	Of the glimpsed moon
akade irinishi	I cannot have my fill; out of sight
sora zo koishiki	Within the skies—there shall all my longing be...

262

Sent to a woman with who I had once spoken, but had not visited in a long time.

おほぶねの上りの綱の綱ゆへに絶ゆとはなくてたゞにやみにし

ōbune no	Great ships are
nobori no tuna no	Upriver hauled by hawsers;
tsuna yue ni	And hawsers
tayu to wa nakute	Never break apart—
tada ni yaminishi	We were merely interrupted!

---

[1] A woman who was referred to as Hyōe no myōbu 兵衛命婦 (Palace Lady Hyōe), is known to have been in service to Fujiwara no Takako (Sonshi) 藤原尊子 (984-1023), one of the consorts of Emperor Ichijō 一条 (980-1011; r. 986-1011), so it seems likely that she is the empress being referred to here.

263

Sent to a lady's house, on an evening when I was serving at the palace.

うちかへし思へばあやし小夜衣九重きつゝたれを戀ふらむ

uchikaeshi	No matter how
omoeba ayashi	I ponder it, 'tis strange:
sayogoromo	My nightshirt[1] — inside out — or
kokonoe kitsutsu	Ninefold garb put on, but for
tare o kouramu	Who, indeed, is my yearning?

264

A woman with whom I had spoken was extremely resentful when I told her I could not visit, so I plucked some broad-leafed bamboo[2] and sent it to her:

かしがまし一夜ばかりの臥しによりなにかは人の猛くうらむる

kashigamashi	How carping!
hitoyo bakari no	Just a single night
fushi ni yori	Spent apart!
nani ka wa hito no	Should it in a lady
takeku uramuru	Arouse such ire?

---

[1] Old Japanese folklore had it that if one wore one's nightclothes inside out, one would dream of one's beloved. 'Ninefold' (*kokonoe* 九重), here is a standard reference to the Imperial Palace. Essentially, Sanekata is saying, 'Whether I'm dressed for work or bed, the only one I dream of is you!'

[2] In his poem Sanekata use the term *kawatake* 河竹, which literally translates as 'river bamboo'. This particular type of bamboo, however, was known for the size of its leaves, and so it was a useful symbol of the, to Sanekata's mind, excessive extent of her complaints. The 'river' also almost certainly recalls the 'river of tears' the lady may have been crying, while he also picks up on the *take* 'bamboo', element in his poem using the adverb *takeku* 猛く 'extremely'.

265

When I went to Usa as messenger, I sent this to a lady's house.

いかにせむ宇佐の使はゆるされず戀しき人はいでの玉水

ika ni semu	What am I to do?
usa no tsukai wa	To go as messenger to Usa
yurusarezu	I am powerless to refuse; yet
koishiki hito wa	The lady I love is
ide no tamamizu	Inconstant as Ide's jewelled waters…[1]

266

When I had gone to the Kiyomizu Temple, I wrote this in the Waterfall Hall.[2]

たきみれどけぶりもたゝず水しあればいかなる熾に水つかるらむ

taki miredo	To strike a spark I've tried, yet
keburi mo tatazu	There's not a wisp of smoke,
mizu shi areba	By dint of the waters;
ika naru oki ni	What embers might lie
mizu tsukaruramu	Beneath the spume?

---

[1] A reference to: 山城の井手の玉水手にむすびたのみしかひもなきよなりけり *yamashiro no / ide no tamamizu / te ni musubi / tanomishi kai mo / naki yo narikeri* 'In Yamashiro / In Ide's jewelled waters / Our hands entwined and / Troth plighted, but to no / Avail.' (*Ise monogatari* 215).

[2] As visitors to Kiyomizu in Kyoto will know, one of the features of the temple grounds is the Otowa waterfall (*otowa no taki* 音羽の滝), although nowadays this has been reduced to three small streams of water. The waters are believed to bring good fortune if you drink them, and were in Sanekata's time, too. The 'Waterfall Hall' (*takidono* 滝殿), rather prosaically, was simply a building near the falls.

267

When I was a dancer at the Lesser Kamo Festival,[1] on passing before the carriage belonging to the ladies of the Kamo Virgin, one of them suddenly called out to me:

行きずりに見つる山井の衣手を

yukizuri ni	As you passed by,
mitsuru yama'i no	I did glimpse indigo, from a peak-
koromode o	born spring
	Staining your sleeves.

And I replied:

めづらしとこそ神はみるらし

mezurashi to koso	Rare is such a thing, indeed!
kami wa mirurashi	Will the gods deign to notice, I wonder?

268

On hearing that a certain lady had become close to another, I wrapped a lotus fruit in a leaf, to make a point of some sort to her.

はちすのみ思ふをいとゞ浮き葉には露にてもなを心をくべし

hachisu nomi	Bitter rue
omou o itodo	You think it not, but how
ukiwa ni wa	Cruel to me, a leaf adrift
tsuyu nite mo nao	On dewdrops; now should
kokoro okubeshi	You pay me heed…

---

[1] An irregular festival at the Kamo Shrine to the north of the capital, held on the Third Day of the Cock in the Eleventh Month.

269

When I was a middle captain, and went as messenger to the Lesser Festival, a woman whom I hand just begun to see, said:

音に聞くこやすべらぎの御垣守

    oto ni kiku   Word has come that
    ko ya suberagi no   Here stands His Majesty's
    mikakimori   Guardsman

I replied:

いとしも戀に夜は燃えねど

    itoshi mo koi ni   Yet not altogether by fires
    yoru wa moenedo   Of nightly passion scorched!

270 .

I had been secretly speaking to woman at the house of the Major Captain of the Right,[1] and when she got pregnant and concealed it:

津の國のたれとふしやのふしかへりそのはらさへやたかくなりしぞ

    tsu no kuni no   In the land of Tsu,
    tare to fushi ya no   With whom have you lain down
    fushikaeri   So well? That
    sonohara sae ya   E'en the meadows—like your
    takakunarishi zo   belly[2]—
          Have been rucked up!

---

[1] A reference to Sanekata's uncle and guardian, Fujiwara no Naritoki 藤原済時.
[2] See poem 178.

271

To a lady named Ben no Kimi,¹ on a night when the moon had shone brightly, when the Consort who was the daughter of the same Major Captain² was serving at the palace:

よそにてもほしとぞきみは思ふらんなにおほぞらの月によそへて

    yoso nite mo   Far away, yet,
hoshi to zo kimi wa   The stars do you
     omouran   Desire, it seems,
 nani ōzora no   While the renowned, heaven-
 tsuki ni yosoete   bound
                              Moon is cloaked…³

272

To the same lady.

影はさぞおぼろけにては見えざらむ寝ぬ夜の月は雲がくれつゝ

    kage wa sazo   The light is as expected:
 oboroke nite wa   Dim, and
   miezaramu   I can see it not;
nenu yo no tsuki wa   On this sleepless night, the moon
kumogakuretsutsu   Is ever hidden 'neath the clouds.

---

[1] The identity of this lady has not been satisfactorily established.
[2] A reference to Fujiwara no Sukeko (Seishi) 藤原娍子 (972-1025), a consort of Emperor Sanjō 三条 (976-1017; r. 1011-1016), and the daughter of Sanekata's uncle, Naritoki.
[3] The translation here is only tentative, as the exact sense remains a mystery to the commentators. Sanekata seems to be suggesting that the lady wants (*hoshi*) the stars (*hoshi*) — a meeting with him — while her mistress — the moon — remains concealed — at the palace.

273

To the same lady.

わかきこが袴の股の絶えしよりそのひさかたのみえぬひぞなき

wakaki ko ga　　　　　A young maiden's
hakama no mata no　　Trousers at the crotch
taeshi yori　　　　　　Did split, and ever since,
sono hisakata no　　　Upon her remote knees has
mienu hi zo naki　　　My gaze been bent!

274

And again:

よる燃ゆるあまのはらをもみてしかばたゞありあけの心ちこそすれ

yoru moyuru　　　　　At night aflame is
ama no hara womo　　The plain of Heaven;
miteshikaba　　　　　Gazing on it that
tada ariake no　　　　'Tis dawn
kokochi koso sure　　I cannot help but feel.

275

And again:

誰か言はむ誰か咎めむあふ事を人よりほかにとまるものかは

tare ka iwamu　　　　Who is it says, and
tare ka togamemu　　Who's is the reproof, that
au koto o　　　　　　We have met?
hito yori hoka ni　　　Is there one other than you
tomaru mono ka wa　To call a halt?

276

And again:

ひたすらにをもひたちにし東地にありけるものかはゞかりの關

hitasura ni	Earnestly
omoi tachinishi	Did I depart
azumaji ni	Upon the eastern roads;
arikeru mono ka	To hesitate before the
habakari no seki	Barrier of Habakari![1]

277

When I heard that a man had gone to the house of a lady I had visited and called himself Sanekata:

あやしくもわが濡れ衣をきたるかな三笠山を人にかられて

ayashiku mo	How strange that
wa ga nureginu o	Faultless, a rain-spattered robe[2]
kitaru kana	I wear;
mikasayama o	My umbrella—a shield—on
hito ni kararete	mount Mikasa[3]
	Was taken by another!

---

[1] The Barrier of Habakari (*habakari no seki* 憚関), was located in Michinoku in the north of Japan. Its primary use in poetry, though was as a play on words, in that *habakari*, also meant 'hesitation'. This poem is, in fact, almost identical to a poem that Sanekata sent back to one of his friends when in Michinoku (218), and demonstrates how a good poet could always adapt a poem for a different situation.

[2] *Nureginu*, which I have translated here as 'a rain-spattered robe', was a standard euphemism for being blamed for something which was not your fault.

[3] Mikasa 三笠 was the name given to one of the three peaks of Mount Kasuga 春日, which lay to the east of Japan's ancient capital, Heijō-kyō 平城京 (modern Nara 奈良). *Kasa* in the place name was homophonous with *kasa* 笠 ('umbrella'), an association which Sanekata uses here.

278

When I had gone to Ishiyama¹ with Middle Captain Nagatō² in the Godless Month,³ looking out at dawn, both the sky and the waters were misted and especially moving, as the plovers called:

冬寒みたつ河霧もあるものをなくなく來居る千鳥かなしな

fuyu samumi	Chill, indeed, is a winter when
tatsu kawagiri mo	Mist rises from the river,
aru mono o	Or so they say;
naku naku ki'iru	Crying, calling, come
chidori kanashi na	The plovers, ever plaintive.

279

At about the time I was made Governor of Michinoku, and was about to withdraw from court, as the pine torches were late in being lit, Middle Captain Michinobu⁴ (with Sanekata) said:

松まつほどぞ久しかりける

matsu matsu hodo zo	Awaiting, our pining time
hisashikarikeru	Has been long, indeed…

And Ko'ōigimi:⁵

みちのくにほど遠ければ武隈の松

michinoku ni	For Michinoku
hodo tōkereba	Is far away as
takekuma no matsu	The pine of Takekuma!⁶

---

[1] A reference to Ishiyamadera 石山寺, a temple on the shores of Lake Biwa 琵琶, to the north-east of the capital.

[2] This is thought to be a reference to Fujiwara no Nagatō/Nagayoshi 藤原長能 (949-1009?), although as he never reached the rank of Middle Captain (*chūjō* 中将), there remains some doubt. Nagatō was a reasonably successful poet, but is now best remembered for taking to his bed and starving himself to death after one of his poems was criticised by Fujiwara no Kintō 藤原公任 (966-1041) at an event hosted by Emperor Kazan.

[3] See poem 48.

[4] See poem 26.

[5] See poem 141.

[6] The pine of Takekuma (*takekuma no matsu* 武隈の松) was a poetic location in Michinoku. It is now said to refer to a spot near Takekoma 竹駒 Shrine in Iwanuma 岩沼, to the south of Sendai 仙台, on Japan's north-eastern coastline, but there is some suspicion that this is simply because of the

280

When I was at the court of the Crown Prince[1] during a Kōshin Rite at the beginning of the year,[2] I composed the following with 'the pointlessness of darkness' as a topic:

にほひさへにほはざりせば梅の花折るにもいかにものうからまし

nioi sae	Had they no scent
niowazariseba	To fragrance them,
mume no hana	Plum blossoms
oru ni mo ika ni	Plucked by touch alone
mono ukaramashi	Would be a chore, indeed!

281

When picking roots of water celery, while at a lady's house:

水深みゝなかくせりと思ふらむあらはれやすき芹にぞありける

mizu fukami	The waters' depths
mina kakuseri to	Conceal all,
omouramu	Or so you think;
arawareyasuki	How plain appears
seri ni zo arikeru	This water celery…

---

similarity between the two names. Its first mention in a poem is in: When he had gone to the province of Michinoku as its governor, he saw a withered pine tree at Takekuma, and had a sapling planted to replace it; after finishing his posting, he returned to the same province later, and saw the pine he had planted once more. 栽し時契やし剣武隈の松をふたたび逢ひ見つる哉 *ueshi toki / chigiri ya si ken / takekuma no / matsu o futatabi / aimitsuru kana* 'When I planted you / Did I make a vow, perhaps? / That Takekuma's / Pine once more / I would encounter!' Fujiwara no Motoyoshi 藤原元善 (GSS XVII: 1241). Referring to the location in a poem thus evoked a hope that one would meet once more, which is what Ko'ōigimi is doing with her contribution here.

[1] Prince Morosada 師貞, the future Emperor Kazan 花山 (968-1008; r. 984-986).
[2] The Kōshin Rite was a periodic religious observance which required people to stay awake all night to ward off illness and ill-luck. This particular one probably took place on the 3rd day of the First Month, Tengen 天元 1 [12.2.978].

282

On hearing that Toki'akira, the Assistant-Governor of Sanuki,[1] had not gone to the house of Koben,[2] in service to the empress.

葛城や一言主もたけからず久米の岩橋渡しはてねば

kazuragi ya	Kazuragi Mountain's
hitokotonushi mo	Master of the Single Word[3]
takekarazu	Lacks courage;
kume no iwabashi	For the boulder bridge of Kume
watashiwateneba	He cannot cross, entirely!

283

When the Imperial Consort from the Koichijō Estate[4] gave birth to her first son,[5] the third night fell upon the fifth day of the Fifth Month.[6]

岩の上のあやめや千代を重ぬらむ今日も五月の五日と思へば

iwa no ue no	Atop the rocks,
ayame ya chiyo o	The sweet-flag will a thousand
kasanuramu	years
kyō mo satsuki no	Endure, no doubt;
itsuka to omoeba	For this day is the Fifth Month's Fifth day, I'm sure.

---

[1] Minamoto no Toki'akira 源時明: he was appointed assistant governor of Sanuki on the 20th day of the First Month Shōryaku 正暦 3 [26.2.992], and held the position until Chōtoku 長徳 1 [995], dating the poem to this period.

[2] The identity of this lady is uncertain, but it is most likely that she was a lady-in-waiting to Empress Sadako (Teishi) 定子 (977-1001).

[3] The Master of the Single Word, *Hitokotonushi no kami* 一言主神, is the deity of Mount Kazuragi, which lies on the border or what are now Osaka and Nara prefectures. He famously slandered the wizard En'nogyōja, who bound him with a spell and commanded him to build a stone bridge between Kazuragi and Kibusen. The bridge remains unfinished to this day, as Hitokotonushi would only work at night, as he was ashamed to be seen in his, hideous, true form. In the poem, of course, Hitokotonushi stands in for Toki'akira, failing to get to the lady's house.

[4] A reference to Sanekata's cousin Seishi (Sukeko) 娍子 (972-1025), the daughter of his uncle Naritoki and a consort to Emperor Sanjō.

[5] Seishi's son was the ill-fated Prince Atsu'akira 敦明 (994-1051) who was unable to ever become emperor as a result of the machinations of Fujiwara no Michinaga.

[6] The Fifth Day of the Fifth Month was the date of the Sweet-flag (*ayame* 菖蒲) festival, when sweet-flags were hung from the eaves of houses in the capital to pray for long life and health. In fact, Sanekata is indulging in some poetic license here, as Atsu'akira was actually born on the 9th day of the Fifth Month.

284

In reply, the Major Captain:[1]

祝ふなる岩のあやめも今日よりは千代のはじめに引きはじむべき

iwau naru	All good things, I pray, for
iwa no ayame mo	This rock-top sweet flag:
kyō yori wa	From this day forth
chiyo no hajime ni	Let a thousand years of fortune
hikihajimubeki	Begin to flow.

285

By the Major Captain, when the Kōshin Rite fell upon the fifth Day of the Fifth Month.[2]

夜のほどのつまとのみなるあやめをもまだ見ぬほどはいつかとぞ思ふ

yo no hodo no	All night long
tsuma to nomi naru	To the eaves wedded is
ayame o mo	A sweet-flag,
mada minu hodo wa	Still unseen,
itsuka to zo omou	But for how long, on this the fifth, I wonder?

286

My reply:

あやめ草寝ぬ夜の空のほとゝぎすまづ曙の聲を聞かばや

ayamegusa	Sweet flag
nenu yo no sora no	Roots: long as a sleepless night sky;
hototogisu	O, Cuckoo!
mazu akebono no	Dawn's first
koe o kikaba ya	Call would I hear!

---

[1] Sanekata's uncle, Fujiwara no Naritoki 済時, grandfather of the infant prince.
[2] The *Kōshin* Rite took place on the Fifth Day of the Fifth Month in Eikan 永観 1 [18.6.983].

287

On the topic of the whiteness of frost at dawn.

霜かとてをきてみつれば月影にみてまがはせる朝ぼらけかな

shimo ka tote	'Is it frost?' I wondered and,
okite mitsureba	Arising, looked
tsukikage ni	Upon the moonlight,
mite magawaseru	But was mistaken,
asaborake kana	On such a dawning.

288

On seeing cormorant fishing boats:

鵜舟さす宇治の川長かずかずにわれのみ嘆く波の上かな

ubune sasu	Poling cormorant boats are
uji no kawa'osa	The men of Uji River;[1]
kazukazu ni	Measureless,
ware nomi nageku	Is my solitary sorrow
nami no ue kana	Atop the waves…

289

なかなかにもの思ひそめて寝ぬる夜はゝかなき夢もえやはみえける

nakanaka ni	In imperfect,
mono'omoisomete	Thought-wracked
nenuru yo wa	Sleep, this night,
hakanaki yume mo	Even a passing dream
e ya wa miekeru	Beyond my sight.

---

[1] Uji lay south-east of the capital, and was a popular location for aristocrats to build villas for an escape from the city. There were a number of poetic locations associated with it, of which the river was the earliest to appear, although it was more common to refer to fishing nets (*ajiroki* 網代木) than cormorant fishing, as Sanekata does here.

290

On seeing underwear[1] hung before a certain lady's chamber, Suketada[2] composed:

むつましき夏の衣をぬぎすてゝいとされがたきあせはじきかな

mutsumashiki	How familiar:
natsu no koromo o	Summer garb
nugisutete	Stripped off and abandoned;
ito saregataki	How difficult to blanch is
asehajiki kana	A sweat-stained chemise!

291

In reply:

いにしへのあまのてこらが織り布も晒せばさるゝものにやはあらぬ

inishie no	Of old
ama no tekora ga	The fisher maidens'
orinuno mo	Woven cloth
saraseba saruru	Could be blanched, if you'd but try it;
mono ni ya aranu	No cause for such commotion!

---

[1] *Asehajiki* 汗弾, which I have translated here as 'underwear', were a type of sleeveless undergarment worn by women to soak up their sweat in the heat of summer. The cloth from which they were made was loosely woven to create a lattice-like effect, and allow perspiration to evaporate from the skin.

[2] Fujiwara no Suketada 藤原輔伊 (?-1021?): little is known about him beyond the fact that he had a number of official appointments, culminating in the position of Director of the Bureau of Carpentry at Junior Fourth Rank, Lower Grade, and he was active in poetic circles, performing in a range of events between 984-1017.

292

On presenting a wig to a certain exalted personage:

君がためやをよのかみをかけつゝもなをすぢごとにいのらるゝかな

kimi ga tame	For you, my lord, upon
yao no kami o	All eight million gods
kaketsutsu mo	I've called, and
nao sujigoto ni	For every strand
inoraruru kana	Have prayed.

293

春風に夜のふけゆけば櫻花散りもやするとうしろめたさに

haru kaze ni	As spring breezes
yo no fukeyukeba	Bring on the night
sakurabana	That the cherry blossoms
chiri mo ya suru to	May fall, or not,
ushirometasa ni	Weighs heavy on my mind.

294

When His Majesty[1] went to view the plum blossom at the Ninna Temple,[2] and was presented with poems by the gentlemen of the court.

散らず待つ花の心も見えぬらしけふよりのちは吹かば吹け風

chirazu matsu	Unscattered and awaiting
hana no kokoro mo	These blossoms' spirit
mienurashi	Have we seen, it seems;
kyō yori nochi wa	From this day forth
fukaba fuke kaze	If you are to blow, then do it, O Wind!

---

[1] Emperor En'yū 円融.

[2] The Ninna Temple (*ninna-ji* 仁和寺) was, and is, located to the north-west of the capital. A Shingon Buddhist temple, it had a close association with the imperial family, as it was founded by Emperor Uda 宇多 (867-931; r. 887-897) in 888. The blossoms of its trees were famously beautiful, and it was a frequent destination for aristocratic excursions.

295

ちぎりてしことの違ふぞたのもしきつらさもかくや變るとおもへば

chigiriteshi
koto no tagau zo
tanomoshiki
tsurasa mo kaku ya
kawaru to omoeba

The promises you made,
Those spoken words, have changed—
On that I can rely;
Your heartless heart, too,
Will it change so, I wonder?

296

After he had made promises to a lady, she told lies about him, so the man:

おぼつかな黒戸に見ゆる菊の花ありてのゝちぞくやしかりける

obotsukana
kurodo ni miyuru
kiku no hana
arite no nochi zo
kuyashikarikeru

Terrible, indeed!
At the back door to the palace, I see
Chrysanthemums:
Past their prime,
I cannot stand them!

297

In reply:

戀しさのさむるよもなきなかなれば夢とぞおもふうつゝならねば

koishisa no
samuru yo mo naki
naka nareba
yume to zo omou
utsutsu naraneba

From love
Awaking—no such nights have we—
Such is our bond, so
All you've heard is but a dream,
Not reality at all…

298

ゆきずりの鈴の音にや群鳥の世をうづらとてなきかくれなむ

yukizure no	Passing by,
suzu no oto ni ya	In the trill of bells,
muradori no	Do the flocking birds
yo o udura tote	Find in this world a cause to quail,
naki kakurenamu	And so hide themselves?

299

When I had been conversing with a lady for some time, I said this to her around the Fourth Month:

卯花の垣根がくれのほとゝぎすわが忍び音といづれほどへぬ

u no hana no	Among the scattered, white deutzia blooms
kakinegakure no	Along the fence concealed is
hototogisu	A cuckoo;
wa ga shinobine to	My plaintive cry, or his,
izure hodo henu	Which has lasted longer?

300

Her reply:

人しれず垣根がくれのほとゝぎすことかたらひて鳴かぬ夜ぞなき

hito shirezu	Unknown to all
kakinegakure no	Along the fence concealed,
hototogisu	The cuckoo
koto kataraite	Has something to say:
nakanu yo zo naki	Not a single night is there he fails to sing!

301

遠へ行きこちこせ川を誰しかも色さりがたき緑染めけむ

<pre>
      ochi e yuki   On its way to distant lands,
  kochikosegawa o   The river Kochikose¹ —
      tare shikamo   Who is it has
      iro sarigataki   A shade of unfading green
   midori somekemu   Stained it?
</pre>

302

そへてわが合はぬ目をさへ嘆くかな物思ふときはまことなりけり

<pre>
     soete wa ga   Indeed, my
   awanu me o sae   Ever-open eyes are
     nageku kana   Full of grief;
  mono'omou toki wa   That I am sunk in sorrow is
    makoto narikeri   True, I tell you.
</pre>

303

When I had gone to a lady's house, I said this, additionally, to her:

妹と寝ば岩戸の空もさし曇りその夜ばかりはあけずもあらむ

<pre>
      imo to neba   When I sleep with my darling,
   iwato no sora mo   That the stone doors of Heaven²
      sashikumori   Should cloud the sky, and
   sono yo bakari wa   This night would never
    akezu mo aramu   Lighten, is my longing.
</pre>

---

[1] The location of this river remains unknown, as references to it have only been posited in two poems in the classical canon. These are: MYS VII: 1112, where the original, Chinese character version of the poem contains a sequence 去来率去河, which was once interpreted as reading *kochikosegawa*, although more recent scholarship now believes it to be *iza isakawa*. The other is this one, which originally occurs in *Saishō chūjō koretada kindachi shunjū uta'awase* 宰相中将伊尹君達春秋歌合 ('The Courtier's Spring and Autumn Poetry Contest held by Consultant Middle Captain Koretada') which took place in the middle of the Seventh Month, Ōwa 応和 3 [963], and also as *Ise-shū* 伊勢集 402.

[2] Sanekata is alluding to the Heavenly Rock Cave, where the sun goddess Amaterasu Ōmikami 天照大神 concealed herself, removing all light from the world. See also poem 85.

304

秋の夜の夜風を寒み吾妹子が衣うつに目を覺ましつゝ

aki no yo no	Autumn night
yokaze o samumi	Winds are so chill;
wagimoko ga	My beloved
koromo utsu ni	Fulling cloth
me o samashitsutsu	Wakes me from my slumber…

305

To Lady Chujō,[1] on the Seventh Day of the Seventh Month.[2]

返さずは程もこそ經れあふ事をいかに貸すべき今日の暮をば

kaesazu wa	Should she not return it,
hodo mo koso Fure	Time would, indeed, pass,
au koto o	Before we could meet again;
ika ni kasubeki	Why would you lend her
kyō no kure o ba	Our meeting on this evening?

306

Her reply:

彦星の心も知らずうちとけてそのあふことを上の空にな

hikoboshi no	Of the Herd Boy's
kokoro mo shirazu	Feelings you know naught!
uchitokete	'tis careless, indeed,
sono au koto o	Our tryst to
ue no sora ni na	The Heavens refuse…

---

[1] This is thought to be the same woman to whom poem 150 is addressed – one of the ladies serving in Fujiwara no Naritoki's mansion.

[2] The festival of Tanabata, when the the celestial lovers, the Herd Boy and the Weaver Maid, met for their annual tryst.

307

After Emperor Kazan had abdicated,¹ I obtained one of the artificial flowers from the Obutsumyō ceremony,² and sent it with this to the house of the Provisional Middle Captain.³

いにしへの色し變らぬものならば花ぞ昔のかたみならまし

inishie no	Their former
iro shi kawaranu	Hues unchanged
mono naraba	Were they to retain,
hana zo mukashi no	Flowers of times long past
katami naramashi	Might be a fitting keepsake.

308

Composed one night when the moon was shining brightly and the Major Captain was playing the zither.⁴

琴の音にあやなく今宵ひかされて月みであかすなげきをやせむ

koto no ne ni	The strains of your zither,
ayanaku koyoi	Alas, this eve
Fikasarete	Are so entrancing, that
tsuki mide akasu	The moon, unwatched, shall set,
nageki o ya semu	I fear…

---

[1] Kazan left the throne on the 23rd day of the Sixth Month Kanna 寛和 2 [1.8.986].

[2] The Obutsymyō (御仏名) ceremony was a court rite carried out from the nineteenth to the twenty-second day of the Twelfth Month every year. Before a screen depicting the horrors of Hell, priests would chant the name of the Buddha in a plea for the court to be pardoned for the sins they had committed during the past year. Part of the decorations for this ceremony were artificial flowers made from wood shavings (*kezuribana* 削り花), and it is one of these that Sanekata has obtained.

[3] This is probably a reference to Fujiwara no Kintō 藤原公任, who is known to have been present at the ceremony in question, but could also be Fujiwara no Michitsuna 藤原道綱.

[4] Sanekata's uncle, Fujiwara no Naritoki (the Major Captain), was noted for his skills on the zither.

309

To someone who passed me by without meeting.

神の杜齋垣の杣にあらねどもいたづらになるくれをいかにせん

kami no mori	The sacred forest precincts,
igaki no soma ni	Walled about with wood,
aranedomo	Never to be among their number,
itazura ni naru	In idleness to no effect
kure o ika ni sen	One evening, what is a plank to do?

310

Composed at court, as a poem with *zo* as the last syllable, on the topic of 'the mountains, dyed in autumn.'

もみぢ葉の色をたづねて入る人も思はぬ山を思ふらむやぞ

momijiba no	Autumn leaves'
iro o tazunete	Colours seeking
iru hito mo	In the mountains, do such folk
omowanu yama o	All unthinking
omouramu ya zo	Dwell on life among the peaks?

311

Composed at court, as a poem with *ko* as the last syllable, on the topic of 'the mountains, dyed in autumn.'

紅葉見て山邊に今日は暮らしてむあればあれそをいもと寝るとこ

momiji mite	Gazing on the autumn leaves
yamabe ni kyō wa	Among the mountains, today
kurashitemu	Let us remain 'til dark;
areba are so o	Heedless of whatever storms may rage,
imo to nuru toko	Such is the bed I share with my love.

312

Dew upon the chrysanthemums.

おぼつかな籬の菊やいかならむ露にをかせてものをこそ思へ

obotsukana How worrying!
magaki no kiku ya The chrysanthemums by yon lattice
ika naramu fence:
tsuyu ni okasete What has befallen them?
mono o koso omoe Covered with dewdrops,
They seem truly sunk in gloomy thoughts.

313

Composed afterwards, on feelings while waiting for the moon to rise at Ide.

もろともに待つべき月を待たずしてひとりも空をながめけるかな

morotomo ni Together
matsubeki tsuki o Should we have awaited the
matazushite moon, yet
hitori mo sora o I could not;
nagamekeru kana In solitude upon the skies
Did you bend your gaze?

314

Around the first day of the Fourth Month,[1] I was somewhat unwell and wrote this to a lady who knew nothing of it, but had sent no letter enquiring.

夏引の糸にはあらず一日より苦しかるとも知らぬなるべし

natsubiki no   Spun in summer
ito[2] ni wa arazu   A silken thread I'm not,
hito hi yori   Yet since the first
kurushikaru to mo   That I have suffered
shiranu narubeshi   You know not, most likely.

Her reply:

繭ごもりふしわづらはゞ夏引のてびきの糸はたえずぞあらまし

mayugomori   Were you cocooned
fushi wazurawaba   Abed and suffering,
natsubiki no   Spun in summer and
tebiki no ito wa   Drawn by hand, a silken thread
taezu zo aramashi   Unending would my concern be…

---

[1] The first day of the Fourth Month (approximately mid-May by our calendar) was the official start of Summer, and the date on which the court changed from warm winter clothing to light and cool summer garb.

[2] *Natsubiki no ito* 夏引の糸, which I have translated here as 'Spun in summer/ A silken thread' was thread drawn from the cocoons of the *harugo* 春蚕 silkworm, which was ready for harvesting at the beginning of summer. Sanekata's reasons for mentioning it are twofold: first, for the connotations of silk cloth and, by association, the light summer clothes the lady will have just changed into; and second, so he can engage in wordplay with the *ito* element, making it part of *ito ni wa arazu* 'not terribly (unwell)' . The lady in her reply reuses *natsubiki no ito*, but in this case she refers to the seeming endless thread of silk drawn from a cocoon as a metaphor for the extent of her concern for Sanekata.

316

Composed on the theme of 'blossoms in the dark in springtime'.

春の夜の闇に心のまどへども殘れる花をいかゞおもはぬ

haru no yo no	In a spring night's
yami ni kokoro no	Dark, my soul
madoedomo	Wanders in confusion, yet
nokoreru hana o	Why, for yon remaining blossoms
ikaga omowanu	Does it lack feeling?

317

Composed on the theme of 'blossoms in the dark in springtime'.

百敷の御垣のうちに春とめて幾千代までの花を見てしか

momoshiki no	Many-stoned
mikaki no uchi ni	The mighty palace walls, and within
haru tomete	Let spring be sealed:
iku chiyo made no	For uncountable ages
hana o miteshika	I would gaze upon these blooms!

318

To a person holding the rank of Crown Prince.[1]

箱鳥のあけてのゝちはなげくとも塒ながらの聲をきかばや

hakodori no	A cuckoo
akete no nochi wa	After dawn is
nagekutomo	A cause for grief;
negura nagara no	While still abed
koe o kikaba ya	Would I hear his call…

---

[1] Prince Okisada/Iyasada 居貞, the future emperor Sanjō 三条 (976-1017; r. 1011-1016).

319

When a lady, with whom I had been conversing secretly, borrowed a pillow from me, I wrote this upon the paper with which I wrapped it.

しるらむとつゝむ枕のほどみればいかにいひてか塵はらふらむ

shiruramu to	Knowing all,
tsutsumu makura no	Discreetly wrapped this pillow is:
hodo mireba	Should it catch another's eye,
ika ni iite ka	How will you explain it?
chiri harauramu	That you were but dusting it, no doubt!

320

Written on seeing a lady with whom I had been conversing in secret on her way to attend at the Palace on a brightly moonlit night.

出づと入ると天つ空なる心地してもの思はする秋の夜の月

izu to iru to	Rising and setting—
ama tsu sora naru	The emptiness of the heavens
kokochi shite	Do I feel, and
mono'omowasuru	Am so sunk in gloom by
aki no yo no tsuki	The moon, upon an Autumn night.

321

On suddenly seeing someone who had lain down to sleep on the bridge,¹ the Provisional Minor Captain, said:

うたゝねの橋とも今宵見ゆるかな

utatane no	'The Bridge of
hashi² to mo koyoi	Fitful Sleep' tonight
miyuru kana	It seems to be!

I replied:

夢路に渡す名にこそありけれ

yumeji ni watasu	Only in dreams across it
na ni koso arikere	Could you go, 'tis said.

322

When my Wet Nurse had taken a bow case, filled it with fruit and sent it off.³

をし張りて弓の袋と知る知るや思はぬ山の物をいるらむ

oshiharite	Greedy, indeed!
yumi no fukuro to	A bow case
shirushiru ya	Did you know it to be, so
omowanu yama no	Why, so thoughtlessly, a mountain
mono o iruramu	Of things did you put within it?

---

[1] Probably the bridge at Uji, famous for its guardian goddess, and a site where Sanekata has previously mentioned dozing, in a similar poetic exchange (poem 57).

[2] This is quite an interesting remark by the Provisional Minor Captain (probably Fujiwara no Michitsuna 藤原道綱), as *utatane no hashi*, here translated as 'the Bridge of Fitful Sleep', is the title of a section in the *Makura no sōshi* ('The Pillow Book'), written by Sei shōnagon, who is known to have been intimate with Sanekata. It suggests that at least some sections of the work were already in circulation at court by this time.

[3] Some versions of the collection's manuscript have 'When the wet nurses had taken a bow case, filled it with fruit, and sent it off to the empress' as a headnote to this poem. Why they would done this, however, remains unclear.

323

聞く人やいかゞ思はむ君によりただ今日ばかり過ぐすと思へど

    kiku hito ya   Folk who hear of it,
   ikaga omowamu   What will they think?
    kimi ni yori   All their trust in you,
   tada kyō bakari   And yet today, at last
   sugusu to omoedo   Did you send it on…

324

雲かゝる峰だに遠きものならば入る夜の月はのどけからまし

    kumo kakaru   Had the cloud covered
   mine dani tōki   Peaks as distant
    mono naraba   Been, then
   iru yo no tsuki wa   The setting moon would
   nodokekaramashi   More tranquil be…

325

On the Seventh Day of the Seventh Month, on a little boat travelling between this world and the Heavens:[1]

天の河かよふ浮木の年を經ていくそかへりの秋をしるらむ

    ama no kawa   The River of Heaven
   kayou ukigi no   Traversing, this raftlet
    toshi o hete   O'er the passing years
   iku so kaeri no   Countless
   aki o shiruramu   Autumns must have known.

---

[1] Sanekata refers to an *ukigi* 浮木, which is a term for a small boat, or raft, but the commentators suggest that he has in mind a boat which made an annual trip between the sea and the Heavens Inukai Kiyoshi, Gotō Shōko and Hirano Yukiko (1994) *Heian Shika Shū*. *Shin Nihon Koten Bungaku Taikei*. Tokyo: Iwanami Shoten.. In his poem, Sanekata is linking this boat's annual trip with the annual crossing of the River of Heaven by the Weaver Maid and the Herd Boy for their annual tryst.

326

人知れぬ仲はうつゝぞなからまし夢さめてのちわびしかりけり

    hito shirenu   A secret
  naka wa utsutsu zo   Affair in real life
    nakaramashi   Is better not;
  yume samete nochi   On waking from my dreams,
   wabishikarikeri   All is lonely sadness.

327

In reply:

夢ならばあはする人もありなましなになかなかのうつゝなるらむ

    yume naraba   If all is a dream, then
  awasuru hito mo   A diviner would
    arinamashi   Show us the way;
  nani nakanaka no   Why, then, does misfortune
  utsutsu naruramu   Dog this reality of ours?

328

When Tadasada, the Governor of Inaba,[1] left for his province:

別れても立ち歸るべき仲なれどいなば戀しと思ふべきかな

wakaretemo	Though we do part, and
tachikaerubeki	Back must go
naka naredo	All that was between us, yet
inaba koishi to	When you are gone to Inaba, fondly
omoubeki kana	Indeed, will you rest in my thoughts.

329

こまほしと思ふ心はありながら勿來の關をつゝまるゝかな

komahoshi to	Of visiting you:
omou kokoro wa	Such thoughts, my heart
arinagara	Do fill, yet
nakoso no seki o	The Barrier at Nakoso[2]
tsutsumaruru kana	Constrains me…

330

おぼつかな世をそむきにし山伏もいかゞあるらむ秋の月をば

obotsukana	I wonder:
yo o somukinishi	Withdrawn from the world,
yamabushi mo	A mountain hermit,
ikaga aruramu	How would he take to
aki no tsuki o ba	This autumn moon?

---

[1] Taira no Tadasada 平忠貞 (Junior Fifth Rank, Upper Grade). He was first appointed Assistant Director of the Bureau of the Palace Kitchen, and then made a Chamberlain in 1011. He was most likely appointed to the post of Governor of Inaba 因幡, a coastal province north-west of the capital region, around the beginning of 1012.

[2] The Barrier of Nakoso (*nakoso no seki* 勿来の関) was a poetic location in Michinoku, referring to the barrier guarding the border between Michinoku and Hitachi provinces. The place name was homophonous with *na ko so* ('Don't come!'), and so the barrier was often mentioned in Love poems with a theme of rejecting a suitor, or of warning one off.

331

When a lady I had been conversing with secretly said, ' My sleeves are chill…'[1]

あふ事のとゞこほるこそわびしけれさゆる袂はとけばとけなむ

au koto no	A tryst with you
todokōru koso	Delayed, would be more
wabishikere	Pitiable by far, for
sayuru tamoto wa	Frozen sleeves
tokeba tokenamu	Once melted, will remain so.

332

When I went to a lady's house, and that night she was not there.

はらふべき友まどはせる鴛鴦も夜半にやなげくけさの朝霜

haraubeki	A mate to brush it from
tomo madowaseru	Him having lost,
oshidori mo	How does the mandarin duck,
yowa ni ya nageku	Grieving through the night,
kesa no asashimo	Face the morning frostfall?

---

[1] A reference to: A poem composed at a competition held by Her Majesty, the Empress during the Kampyō era (889-898). ゆふされば螢よりけにもゆれどもひかりみねばや人のつれなき *sasa no Fa ni / woku shimo yori mo / hitori nuru / wa ga koromode zo / saemasarikeru* 'On bamboo grass leaves / Settles frost, but / Sleeping alone, / My sleeves / Are colder still by far.' Ki no Tomonori 紀友則 (KKS XII: 563).

333

When the Minister of the Right[1] mentioned, '…as the moon across the skies'.[2]

ちぎりあらば旅の空なるほどばかりすぐる月日も心あらなむ

<blockquote>

chigiri araba	If 'tis my fate, then
tabi no sora naru	While under journey's skies
hodo bakari	I spend my time,
suguru tsuki hi mo	With the passing of the days and months
kokoro aranamu	Let me rest within your heart.

</blockquote>

334

At Gosechi time,[3] when snow fell and then quickly vanished.

淡雪のふるほどもなく消えぬるは明日のひかげやかねてさすらむ

<blockquote>

awayuki no	A froth of snow
furu hodo mo naku	Fallen and then in no time
kienuru wa	Gone:
asu no hikage ya	Was it that the morrow's sunlight[4]
kanete sasuramu	Had already shone?

</blockquote>

---

[1] Most likely to have been Fujiwara no Michinaga 藤原道長 at this time.

[2] Michinaga is quoting a well-known poem: When Tachibana no Tadamoto had been seeing someone's daughter in secret, he sent this to her to tell her he was going far away. 忘るなよほどは雲居になりぬとも空行く月のめぐりあふまで *wasuru na yo / hodo wa kumoi ni / narinu tomo / sora yuku tsuki no / meguri au made* 'Forget me not! / For though the heavens' span / May part us / As the sky-bound moon / Circles we shall meet again.' Tachibana no Tadamoto (SIS VIII: 470).

[3] *Gosechi* refers here to the Feast of New Grain (*toyo no akari no sechie* 豊明節会), which took place immediately after the New Rice Festival (*niinamesai* 新嘗祭), a court event where the emperor made the first offering of that year's new rice to the gods in the Eleventh Month of the year.

[4] A reference to the Gosechi festival, in that the cords used to bind one's hair for the occasion were known as *hikage no kami* 日蔭の髪. 'sunlight hair'.

335

いかにせむ久米路の橋の中空に渡しも果てぬ身とやなりなむ

ika ni semu What I am to do? For as
kumeji no hashi no The Bridge of Kumeji,[1]
nakazora ni In mid-air
watashi mo hatenu Unable to complete my crossing,
mi to ya narinamu Am I to become?

336

別るとも衣の關のなかりせば袖濡れましや都ながらも

wakaru tomo Though I shall depart,
koromo no seki no The Barrier at Koromo[2]
nakariseba Is not upon me yet, so
sode nuremashi ya Should my sleeves be so soaked,
miyako nagara mo While I am yet in the Capital?

---

[1] See poem 107.
[2] See poem 185.

337

On the first day of the Eighth Month, after His Majesty, Retired Emperor Kazan had given me a bow, and the day when I had to depart was delayed, as if to say, 'When is it that you're really off?'[1] His Majesty said:

言へばあり言はねば苦しわかれぢを

ieba ari	When I say, 'Farewell', you linger
iwaneba kurushi	on, but
wakareji o	To leave it unsaid, a painful
	Parting, it would be…

And I sadly replied:

そのほどゝだにいかできこえじ

sono hodo to dani	If only the appointed date, I could,
ika de kikoeji	Somehow, leave unmentioned…

---

[1] Sanekata was appointed to the post of Governor of Michinoku on the 13th day of the First Month Chōtoku 長徳 1 [15.2.995], but did not leave the capital to take up his duties until 27th day of the Ninth Month of the same year [23.10.995]. The bow from Kazan was a farewell gift, and he was obviously expecting Sanekata to be leaving soon after receiving it.

338

Going to the New Rice Festival[1] in the evening, a lady's face was open to view, so I concealed it with my sleeves; on descending from the cart, she said:

ひかげかくしゝ袖ぞわすれぬ

hikage kakushishi   Garlanded with sunlight vine, and
sode zo wasurenu   hidden by
     Those sleeves, I never shall forget…

I replied:

おほぞらのくもの浮きたる身なれども

ōzora no   Within the boundless skies,
kumo no ukitaru   A drifting cloud[2]
mi naredomo   Is my state, yet…

339

I was unable to meet with a lady, with whom I had been conversing, for some time due to a hindrance, and hearing that she had said I was probably unwell:

あやなわが思ひわづらふこともなしあはぬばかりや苦しかるらむ

aya na wa ga   Absurd, indeed! I
omoi wazurau   For suffering
koto mo nashi   Have no cause;
awanu bakari ya   Not meeting you, is all
kurushikaruramu   That would bring me pain…

---

[1] See poem 58.

[2] A cloud, of course, has no fixed abode in the sky, and by comparing himself to one, Sanekata is telling the lady he has no definite residence, and hence no formal wife, as custom had it that men lived in the home of their principal wife.

340

春くれど春に知られぬむもれ木は花みる人をよそにこそ聞け

haru kuredo	Spring is come, yet
haru ni shirarenu	Knowing nothing of it
mumoregi wa	A blackened, buried tree,
hana miru hito o	The folk gone blossom viewing
yoso ni koso kike	In the distance hears.

341

Sent to the Crown Prince,[1] from the Provinces, around the Fifth Month.

はるかなる深山がくれのほとゝぎす聞く人なしにねをやなくらむ

harukanaru	In the distant
miyamagakure no	Mountains' heart hidden
hototogisu	Would the cuckoo,
kiku hito nashi ni	With no one to hear
ne o ya nakuramu	Cry out his call?

342

When the Captain of the Outer Palace Guards[2] said, 'Of no account, I would even my heart…'[3]

つらきにし人の命のながらへばうらみられてもよをやつくさむ

tsurakinishi	If by a heartless
hito no inochi no	Girl, life
nagaraeba	Would be prolonged…
uramiraretemo	But will despite alone,
yo o ya tsukusamu	Exhaust a man's allotted span?

---

[1] Prince Okisada/Iyasada 居貞, the future Emperor Sanjō 三条 (976-1017; r. 1011-1016).
[2] Probably a reference to Fujiwara no Kintō 藤原公任 (966-1041).
[3] Kintō is quoting: Topic unknown. 數ならぬ身は心だになから南思しらずは怨ざるべく *kazu naranu / mi wa kokoro dani / nakaranan / omoishirazu wa / uramizarubeku* 'Of no account, / I would even my heart / Were gone, / Then, all unknowing / I'd not despise you so…' Anonymous (SIS XV: 984) here, and Sanekata's offering should be read as a reply to it.

343

While I was in the province of Michinoku, and had not heard a cuckoo call, I sent this to a lady around the Fifth Month.

みやこには聞きふりぬらむほとゝぎす關のこなたの身こそつらけれ

miyako ni wa	In the capital, you
kikifurinuramu	Must be accustomed to hearing
hototogisu	Cuckoos;
seki no konata no	This side of the barrier,
mi koso tsurakere	Am I left, all forlorn.

344

Her reply:

ほとゝぎす勿來の關のなかりせば君が寢覺めにまづぞ聞かまし

hototogisu	A cuckoo,
nakoso no seki no	Were the hindering barrier of
nakariseba	Nakoso[1]
kimi ga nesame ni	Gone,
mazu zo kikamashi	On waking, my Lord,
	Would be the first sound to your ears.

345

Her reply:

君來ずは死出山にぞほとゝぎすしばし勿來の關をすゑまし

kimi kozu wa	With you not come, my Lord,
shidenoyama ni zo	Upon the Mount of Shide will
hototogisu	The cuckoos
shibashi nakoso no	A while by Nakoso
seki o suemashi	Barrier halted be.

---

[1] The lady is engaging in a familiar wordplay here as the place name Nakoso 勿來, the location of one of the barriers between Michinoku and the capital, was homophonous with *na ko so* な來そ, meaning 'Come not!'

346

On the Seventh Day of the Seventh Month, on the feelings of the Weaver Maid at parting:

別るれど待ては頼もしたなばたのこのよに逢はぬ仲をいかにせむ

wakaruredo   Though they must part
mateba tanomoshi   If she but waits, trust can
tanabata no   The Weaver Maid;
kono yo ni awanu   Unmet this night,
naka o ikani semu   What is to become of us…

347

吾妹子がゝづけし綿を取らぬかとみるまで照らす菊の上の露

wagimoko ga   My beloved has the blooms
kazukeshi wata o   Capped with cotton;
toranu ka to   I'll not take it
miru made terasu   Until within my gaze shines
kiku no ue no tsuyu   Dewfall, atop the chrysanthemums.

348

君戀ふる涙やきりてかくしけむひとり寝る夜の月なかりしは

kimi kouru   Yearning for you, my eyes with
namida ya kirite   Tears are fogged and
kakushikemu   Blinded
hitori nuru yo no   Sleeping all alone tonight
tsuki nakarishi wa   The Moon was lost to view.

References

Arntzen S (1997) *The Kagerō Diary*. Ann Arbor: Center for Japanese Studies University of Michigan.

Goodwin JR (2007) *Selling Songs and Smiles: The Sex Trade in Heian and Kamakura Japan*. Honolulu: University of Hawai'i Press.

Inukai Kiyoshi, Gotō Shōko and Hirano Yukiko (1994) Heian Shika Shū. *Shin Nihon Koten Bungaku Taikei*. Tokyo: Iwanami Shoten.

Kubota Jun and Baba Akiko (1999) Uta kotoba uta makura daijiten. In: Kubota Jun and Baba Akiko (eds) *Uta kotoba uta makura daijiten*. Tokyo: Kadokawa Shoten.

McAuley TE (2020a) *The Poetry Contest in Six Hundred Rounds: A Translation and Commentary*. Leiden: Brill.

McAuley TE (2020b) The Power of Translation: Issues in the translation of premodern Japanese waka. *Waseda RILAS Journal* 8: 1-19.

McMillan P (2010) *One Hundred Poets, One Poem Each: A Translation of the Ogura Hyakunin Isshu*. New York: Columbia University Press.

Sei Shōnagon (2006) *The Pillow Book*. London: Penguin Books.

Seidensticker EG (1964) *The Gossamer Years (Kagero Nikki) The Diary of a Noblewoman of Heian Japan*. Tokyo: Charles E. Tuttle Co.

Watson F (2020) *One Hundred Leaves: A new annotated translation of the Hyakunin Isshu*. Plum White Press.

Index

A

Akazome emon, 112
amanogawa, 13
Amaterasu ōmikami, 50, 59, 147
Amida, 20, 99
aouma no sechie, 50
Ariwara no
    Narihira, vi, 37
asahiyama, 12
ausaka, 92, 96
Awa, 83
Awata Palace, 17

B

Biwa Mansion, 62
Buzen, 1

C

Captain of the Outer Palace Guards, 129
Chang'an, iii
Chikuzen, 1
courtiers' hall. *See* tenjō no ma
cuckoo. *See* hototogisu

D

Dance and Song Festival, 50
Director of the Bureau of the Palace Guards. *See* Fujiwara no Kintō

E

Eiga Monogatari, 62
Emperor
    En'yū, 8, 9, 10, 15, 16, 43, 48, 76, 95, 118, 125, 144
    Ichijō, 48, 130
    Kazan, 15, 17, 23, 41, 45, 55, 87, 138, 139, 149, 162
    Ōjin, 1
    Saga, 26
    Sanjō, 21, 98, 110, 135, 140, 153, 164
    Sujin, 55
    Tenmu, 90
    Uda, 144
    Yūryaku, 60
Empress
    Jingū, 1
En'nogyōja, 60, 140
evening cicada. *See* higurashi

F

Feast of New Grain, 50
Fujiwara no
    Akiko (Senshi), 48, 125
    Asamitsu, 99
    Kagemasa, 14
    Kane'ie, 17, 20
    Kintō, 74, 108, 129, 138, 149, 164
    Kuninori, 14
    Michikane, 17, 42
    Michinaga, 20, 33, 59, 129, 140, 160
    Michinobu, 16, 17, 18, 23, 29, 43, 46, 92, 138
    Michitaka, 42
    Michitsuna, 20, 23, 56, 57, 65, 86, 87, 149, 155
    Morotada, v
    Nagatō/Nagayoshi, 138
    Nagayori, 30

Naritoki, v, 4, 6, 7, 25, 27, 30, 40, 49, 54, 55, 62, 80, 92, 99, 100, 104, 105, 134, 135, 140, 141, 148, 149
Nobuko (Junshi), 118
Norikane, vi, 112
Noriko (Senshi), 95
Sadako (Teishi), 83, 140
Sadatoki, v
Sanekata, iv, v, vi, vii, ix, 1, 3, 4, 6, 7, 8, 9, 11, 12, 13, 15, 16, 19, 20, 23, 25, 27, 28, 29, 30, 31, 33, 35, 36, 37, 39, 40, 42, 43, 45, 46, 47, 48, 49, 50, 52, 53, 54, 55, 58, 59, 62, 65, 66, 67, 75, 76, 78, 79, 80, 86, 88, 89, 90, 92, 93, 95, 96, 98, 99, 100, 101, 104, 106, 107, 110, 113, 115, 116, 117, 119, 120, 121, 126, 127, 128, 129, 131, 132, 134, 135, 137, 138, 140, 141, 142, 147, 149, 152, 155, 156, 162, 163, 164
Sanemasa, 104
Sanesuke, 42
Sukeko (Seishi), 25, 135
Suketada, 143
Suketō, 116
Tadako (Shishi), 55
Taka'ie, 108
Takako (Sonshi), 130
Tamemasa, 3
Tametō, 27, 30, 42, 44, 52, 53
Teika, iv
Teruko (Kōshi), 8, 76
Yasusuke, 112
Yoshichika, 34
fukiage, 127
furu no yashiro, 55
fushimi, 39
futami no ura, 67

G

ganjitsu no sechie, 50
Genji monogatari, vi, 14, 24
Godless Month. *See* kaminazuki

Gosechi, 39, 50, 84, 90, 160
Great Purification Ceremony, 38

H

habakari, 111, 137
Hachiman, 1, 3
hagi, 24, 115
hakokata, 109, 110
Hall of Bright Proclamations, 91, 95, 109
Hall of Broad Beauty. *See* Kokiden
Hall of Received Fragrance, 55
harimagata, 98
Hasedera, 119
hashihime, 14, 31, 102
Hatsuse, 119
hayami, 57, 83, 127
Heian-kyō, iii
higurashi, 5, 93
hitokotonushi, 124, 140
Hitokotonushi, 60, 140
Hitokotonushi no kami, 60
Horikawa Palace, 8
hototogisu, 4, 6, 35, 41, 42, 57, 68, 74, 81, 82, 98, 114, 125, 141, 146, 164, 165
 nakubeki eda to, 23
Hyōe no myōbu. *See* Lady Hyōe

I

ibuki, 67, 126
iki no matsubara, 1
inaba, 54, 158
Isonokami, 55
Iwashimizu Hachiman Shrine, 3

J

jōkyōden. *See* Hall of Received Fragrance
Junior Assistant Handmaid, 125

K

Kagerō nikki, 20
kamakurayama, 35

kaminazuki, 27, 59
Kasama, 30
Kasuga, 22, 56, 137
katsuragawa, 3, 126
Kawashiri, 59
Kazuragi, 60, 140
Ki no Tsurayuki, iii
Kin'yōwakashū, 52
Kingyokushū, 74
Kiyomizu, 132
Kiyowara no
    Motosuke, 94
Ko'ōigimi, 52, 53, 76, 138, 139
Ko'ōigimi-shū, 52, 53
kochikosegawa, 147
Kogawa, 127
Koichijō, 6, 40, 49, 54, 100, 106, 140
kokiden, 33
Kokinwakashū, iii
Koma no Myōbu, 8
koromo no seki, 96, 99, 161
Kōshin, 6, 23, 58, 139, 141
Koshirakawaden. *See* Shirakawa
Kosogimi, 25
Kumano, 87
Kume, 124, 140
kumeji, 60, 161
kurahashiyama, 98

L

Lady
    Ben no Kimi, 135
    Chujō, 148
    Chūjō, 80
    Emon, 100, 106
    Hyōe, 130
    Jijū, 62
    Koben, 83, 140
    Kojijū, 48, 95
    Koma no Myōbu, 8, 48
    Saishō, 53, 83, 91, 95
    Sako, 85
    Shōjō, 50, 102
    Suri, 54
Lesser Kamo Festival, 133

M

Major Captain. *See* Fujiwara no
    Naritoki
Major Captain of the Right. *See*
    Fujiwara no Naritoki
makura kotoba, vii, 32
Makura no sōshi, 27, 53, 83, 155
Matsushima, 86
Meeting Hill. *See* ausaka
Michinoku, v, vi, 86, 92, 96, 99, 100,
    108, 109, 111, 112, 113, 125, 137,
    138, 158, 162, 165
mikasayama, 137
Mikawa, 37, 58
Minamoto no
    Masazane, v
    Michikata, 39
    Mitsunaka, 66
    Nobukata, 27, 28, 31, 32, 97, 107,
        111
    Nobumitsu, 49
    Shigenobu, 27
    Taka'akira, 19
    Tamesuke, 35, 36, 42, 74
    Toki'akira, 140
    Tsunefusa, 19
    Yorimitsu, 100
Mishima, 48, 60
Mistress of His Majesty's Breakfast.
    See Naizen no myōbu
Mitoshigawa, 111
miwa, 80
Miyanome Festival, 30
Mount Kamakura. *See* kamakurayama
Murasaki Shikibu, vi
murasakino, 15
muro no yashima, 52, 53
musashino, 89

N

Nagara, 26
Naizen no myōbu, 11
nakagawa, 95
nakoso no seki, 158, 165
Nara, 22, 55, 80, 98, 128, 137, 140
narabi no oka, 11

natsu koromo
    usukinagara zo, 121
natsubiki no ito, 152
New Year Festival, 50
Night Attendants' Offices. *See*
    tonoidokoro
niinamesai, 32, 160
Nijō Major Controller of the Left. *See*
    Minamoto no Tamesuke
Ninna Temple, 144
Nishikawa, 20
nomori, 47

O

Obutsumyō ceremony, 149
Ōe no
    Masahira, 112
Ogura hyakunin isshu, iv
Ōhara, 56, 57
ōigawa, 79, 126
Ōnaobi no kami, 31
Onoyama, 17
oshidori, 117, 159
oshio, 44
otowa no taki, 132
Ou, 91

P

Palace Handmaid, 55
Prince
    Atsu'akira, 140
    Morosada, 139
    Okisada/Iyasada, 21, 25, 98, 110, 153, 164
Princess
    Sukeko (Shishi), 10
Provisional Minor Captain. *See*
    Fujiwara no Michitsuna

R

River Katsura. *See* katsuragawa
Rokujō Minor Counselor. *See*
    Minamoto no Michikata

S

Saigyō, vi
Sakurai, 13, 98
Sei shōnagon, 27, 28, 53, 83, 94, 155
sen'yōden, 25, 91
Serving Girl
    Kokonoe, 92
    Seki, 92
Settsu, 6
shikashū, iv
Shikitsu, 6
Shinano, 93
Shirakawa, 4, 5, 7, 46, 92, 109, 113
shirakawa no seki, 92
Shūiwakashū, vi, 19, 20, 74, 76
sonohara, 93
Sukunami no Kami, 30
sumaigusa, 40
Sweet-Flag Festival, 50

T

Taira no
    Tadasada, 158
    Takako, 118, 120
takekuma no matsu, 138
tamuin, 24
tanabata, 25, 53, 58, 68, 76, 85, 103, 166
tango no sechie, 50
tenjō no ma, 35
tōchi, 128
tōka no sechie, 50
tokonatsu, 71, 107, 115
tonoidokoro, 76
tonomoryō, 89
toyo no akari no sechie, 50, 84, 90, 160
toyooka hime, 59
Tsu, 87
Tsutsugimi, 86, 113

U

uguisu, 23, 61
Uji, 3, 12, 14, 20, 31, 102, 142, 155
Urashima Tarō, 18, 65
Usa, 1, 30, 74, 75, 116, 132

utamakura, vii, 6, 11, 12, 13, 67, 91, 109, 125, 128

W

waka, iii, iv, vii, viii, x, 67
Weaver Maid. *See* tanabata

White Horse Banquet, 50

Y

Yamashiro, 11, 96, 128, 132
yatsuhashi, 37
yūdasuki, 12

Index of First Lines

adanami no, 48
agemaki ya, 78
aiomowanu, 122
akazarishi, 16
akegataki, 67
akenu yo no, 69
aki hatenu, 101
aki hatete
    augi kaesu wa, 101
    kami no shigure mo, 47
aki kaze no
    fuku ni chirikau, 13
    sayo fukegata ni, 119
aki no no ni, 24
aki no yo ni, 41
aki no yo no, 148
aku made mo, 18
ama no kawa, 156
ama no to o
    ake chō koto o, 51
    sashite koko ni to, 51
    wa ga tame ni to wa, 50
amanogawa
    kayou ukigi ni, 13
    momiji o hashi ni, 13
amata tabi, 104
ame ni masu, 30
asahiyama, 12
asakura ya, 69
ashi no kami, 33
ashi no ya no, 94
au koto no, 159
au koto o, 127
awanu ma no, 128

aware chō, 123
awayuki no, 160
aya na wa ga, 163
ayamegusa, 141
ayashiku mo, 137
azumaji no, 108
chigiri araba, 160
chigiri arite, 79
chigiriteshi, 145
chikaiteshi, 71
chirazu matsu, 144
eda kawasu, 22
eji ga ishi, 9
fuku kaze ni, 113
fuku kaze no, 11
fune nagara, 6
futaba yori, 60
fuyu samumi, 138
ha o shigemi, 5
habukitsutsu, 114
hachisu nomi, 133
hachisuba ni, 77
hakodori no, 153
hama chidori, 116
hana no ka ni, 17
haraubeki, 159
haru kaze ni, 144
haru kori no, 27
haru kuredo, 164
haru no yo no, 153
harukanaru, 164
hashihime ni
    sodekata shikinamu, 14
    yowa no samosa mo, 14
hashihime no, 102
hikage kakushishi, 163
hikage sasu, 91
hikoboshi no
    kokoro mo shiranu, 103

kokoro mo shirazu, 148
kubeki yoi to ya, 77
hiro bakari, 78
hiromae ni, 31
hisakata no, 130
hitasura ni, 137
hito shirenu, 157
hito shirezu
    kaereru koto o, 120
    kakinegakure no, 146
hito sirezu, 105
hitori nomi, 69
honobono ni, 93
hototogisu, 23
    hana tachibana no, 81
    nakoso no seki no, 165
idetachite, 28
ieba ari, 162
iite nazo, 15
ika de ka wa
    hito no kayowanu, 92
    omoi ari to wa, 52
ika nareba, 51
ika narishi, 119
ika ni semu
    kumeji no hashi no, 161
    usa no tsukai wa, 132
ikanaru, 32
ima wa tote, 61
imo to neba, 147
inishi fuyu, 58
inishie mo, 124
inishie no
    ama no tekora ga, 143
    aoi to hito ga, 72
    iro shi kawaranu, 149
    katami ni kore ya, 107
    koromo no iro no, 29
    tane to shi mireba, 4
    yama'i no mizu ni, 29
inishie o, 113
inochi dani, 102
isa ya mada, 30
ise ono ya, 120
iso no kami, 118, 119
isoganamu, 129
isogazu wa, 28
itsu to naku, 27

iwa no ue no, 140
iwaba ie, 71
iwau naru, 141
izu to iru to, 154
izure o ka, 77
kaeru kari, 106
kaesamu to, 19
kaesazu wa, 148
kage ni dani, 10
kage wa sazo, 135
kakikumori, 35
kakikurashi, 118
kakotsubeki, 89
kaku namu to, 79
kaku to dani, 67
kakurenaki, 91
kakushi koso, 75
kami no mori, 150
kamimaishi, 50
kano hitsu wa, 42
karakoromo, 37
karenikeru, 73
kari narade, 57
kashigamashi, 131
katazu makezu no, 40
katsuragawa, 3
kaze fukanu, 70
kaze hayami
    arashi no yama no, 83
    fukiage no hama no, 127
kaze no ma ni, 12
kaze o itami
    funadeshi noda no, 125
    motoara no hagi no, 115
kazoureba, 36
kazu naranu, 164
kazukazu ni, 97
kazuragi ya, 140
keburi tatsu, 88
kigisu naku, 56
kigisu sumu, 44
kiku hito ya, 156
kimi ga tame, 144
kimi ga yado, 98
kimi kouru, 166
kimi kozu wa, 165
ko wa sara ni, 117
koisemahoshiki, 37

koishisa no, 145
koishitomo, 126
koko nagara, 128
kokonoe ni, 8
kokonoe wa, 92
kokoro ni mo, 110
kokoro usa no, 74
koma ni ya wa, 48
komahoshi to, 158
kono goro wa, 53
kono haru wa
    ikade mutsuren, 99
    iza yamazato ni, 17
    mezurashigenaki, 88
kore o miyo, 63
kore ya kono, 87
koshi michi ni, 75
koto no ne ni, 149
kototetemu, 108
kuchi mo senu, vi
kumo kakaru, 156
kumo no ue o, 39
kumoi nite, 106
kurahashi no, 98
kure ni mo to, 126
kyō kyō to, 117
kyō yori wa
    hitoe ni tanomu, 123
    tsuyu no inochi mo, 5
madoromanu, 70
mae kata no, 34
matazu koso, 68
matsu matsu hodo zo, 138
matsu ni koso, 86
mayugomori
    fushi wazurawaba, 152
    oya no kau ko no, 72
me no mae ni
    mazu mo wasururu, 100
    taesezu miyuru, 100
mi ni chikaki, 65
mi no naramu, 100
michinoku ni, 96
mika no yo no, 49
mikaki yori, 9
mimu to iishi, 46
minu hodo no, 109
mitsu to nomi, 80

miyako ni wa
    kikifurinuramu, 165
    tare o ka kimi wa, 112
miyakobito, 4
mizu fukami, 139
mizukaki no, 66
mizukara wa, 104
momiji mite, 150
momijiba no, 23, 150
momoshiki no, 153
mono o dani, 57
morotomo ni
    matsubeki tsuki o, 151
    okifushi mono o, 71
    okuru ashita mo, 84
mube shi koso, 114
mukashi mishi, 1
murasaki no
    hito moto yue ni, 89
    iro ni idekeru, 90
    kumo no tanabiku, 43
murasakino, 15
musubu chō, 54
musubu te no
    shizuku ni nigoru, 54, 122
    wakare to omou ni, 116
mutsumashiki, 143
nagamuru o, 127
nakagawa ni, 95
nakanaka ni, 142
nami no yoru, 20
nani ni ka wa, 99
nani o shite, 59
nani semu ni, 52
natsu koromo, 121
natsubiki no, 152
nioi sae, 139
nodoka ni mo, 45
obotsukana
    ika ni ware semu, 90
    kakaranu tabi mo, 66
    kurodo ni miyuru, 145
    mada akenu yo no, 82
    magaki no kiku ya, 151
    ware kotozukeshi, 57
    yo o somukinishi, 158
    yumeji no ono no, 62
ōbune no, 130

ochi e yuki, 147
ōigawa, 79
ōkata wa, 62
okite miba, 76
okite miru, 78
omigoromo, 63
omoe kimi, 117
omou koto, 21
oshiharite, 155
oshio yama, 44
osoku tomo, 18
oto ni kiku, 134
ou no ura ni, 91
oya mo ko mo, 26
ōzora no, 28
sagoromo ni, 122
saoshika no, 38
sasagani no, 64
satsuki yami, 98
shima no ko wa, 65
shimo ka tote, 142
shinobine mo, 125
shinobine no, 82
shirakawa ni, 7
shirakumo no, 109
shiranedomo, 89
shiratsuy no, 90
shirazushite, 86
shiruramu to, 154
shita ni nomi, 89
soete mata, 105
soete wa ga, 147
sonohara ya, 93
su no uchi ni, 97
sumizome no, 16
ta ga sato ni, 42
ta ga tame ni, 41
tachiyoramu, 11
tadachi ni wa, 54
taene to ya, 95
take no wa ni, 64
taki miredo, 132
tamakushige, 18
tanabata ni, 53
tanabata no, 58
   kesa no wakare ni, 25
   kokochi koso sure, 68
   morote ni isogu, 76

o ni nuku tama mo, 85
tanabata wa, 103
tare ka iwamu, 136
tare naramu, 47
tare zo kono, 80
taso ya kono, 121
tatsu kiji no, 43
toki wa haru, 22
tokonatsu no, 115
tomaru ya to, 114
tomete dani, 81
toshi o hete, 123
tsu no kuni no, 134
tsukikage mo, 111
tsukikage o, 45
tsunenaranu, 24
tsurakinishi, 164
tsuyu harau, 129
u no hana no, 146
ubune sasu, 142
uchikaeshi, 131
ueshi toki, 139
uete miru, 10
uguisu no, 61
uji gawa no, 31
ujigawa no, 20
uki koto ni, 81
uki ni kaku, 104
uki yo ni wa, 46
ura kaze ni, 83
ushirometa, 124
usushi to ya, 107
utatane no
   hashi to mo koyoi, 155
   kono yo no yume no, 26
wa ga goto ya, 60
wa ga io wa, 80
wa ga tame ni, 21
wa o shigemi, 93
wagimoko ga, 166
wakaki ko ga, 136
wakareji no, 110
wakareji wa, 108
wakaretemo, 158
wakaru tomo
   koromo no seki no, 161
   wakare mo hateji, 75
wakaruredo, 166

ware nagara, 56
warinashi ya, 55
wasurarenu, 112
wasurezu yo, 94
wasuru na yo, 160
yado no ue ni, 6
yae nagara, 8
yamabito no
　　ono no e wa mina, 85
　　ono no tayori to, 63
yamashiro no, 132
yamazato ni, 74
yasurawazu, 111
yo no hodo no, 141
yoru moyuru, 136
yoso ni kaku, 55
yoso nite mo, 135
yū kakete, 84
yukiyarade, 59
yukizure no, 146
yukizuri ni, 133
yume naraba, 157
yūnagi ni, 87

www.ingramcontent.com/pod-product-compliance
Lightning Source LLC
Chambersburg PA
CBHW061323040426
42444CB00011B/2743